EDITOR IN CHIEF®

Book C2 Grammar Disasters and Punctuation Faux Pas

SERIES TITLES:

Editor in Chief® A1 • Editor in Chief® B1 • Editor in Chief® C1

Editor in Chief® A2 • Editor in Chief® B2 • Editor in Chief® C2

Created by Michael Baker

Written by Carrie Beckwith, Cheryl Block, Margaret Hockett, & David White

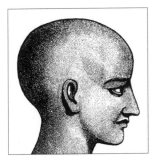

© 1999

CRITICAL THINKING BOOKS & SOFTWARE

www.criticalthinking.com

P.O. Box 448 • Pacific Grove • CA 93950-0448

Phone 800-458-4849 • FAX 831-393-3277

ISBN 0-89455-721-1

Printed in the United States of America

TABLE OF CONTENTS

TO THE TEACHER

Objective

Editor in Chief® reinforces the rules of written English by providing the student with practice in editing a variety of formats. Students develop a basic understanding of the rules of grammar and mechanics in context and exercise their critical thinking abilities by identifying content errors. Book A covers the skills generally taught in grades 4–6, Book B covers those taught in grades 6–8, and Book C covers skills for grades 8 and up.

Rationale

The key difference between *Editor in Chief®* and most grammar series is the focus on editing in context. The grammatical and mechanical errors inserted into the activities are based on general instructional guidelines for specific grade levels; the content level, however, remains ungraded, allowing usage of these materials at many instructional levels. Styles and content are varied to sustain interest and broaden the student's exposure to different writing formats such as letters, directions, schedules, and dialogue. The illustrations integrated into the context of the activities further spark student interest. The editing skills developed can be applied to the student's own writing.

Activity

Each activity consists of at least one content error (a discrepancy between the illustration/caption and the writing sample) and 13–18 errors in spelling, mechanics, and grammar. The student must identify these errors and make appropriate corrections. An editing checklist, included on page ix of this book, may be used by the student to aid in the editing task. Most corrections involve the insertion, modification, or deletion of punctuation marks, capitals, and single words and short phrases within the text. Some corrections will involve rewriting of single sentences. Each writing sample is based on an accompanying illustration and caption. Information in the illustration and caption is correct (content errors occur only where the story is *contradicted* by the illustration or caption). The student may insert corrections and recopy the corrected article. Activities are sequenced according to type, number, and level of errors and also by complexity of subject matter.

Using the Answer Key

The answer key (p. 35) lists corrections for each article. Each numbered correction is followed by a shorthand explanation of the error type and a bracketed reference to the specific rule in the Grammar Guide (p. 81). The teacher may give students the number and type of errors prior to editing. A student may be able to correct an error in more than one way. The answer key gives some obvious choices, but the teacher may accept other answers that make sense and are grammatically and mechanically correct.

Teaching Suggestions

Editor in Chief® can be used as an individual or group activity for instruction, reinforcement, practice, and assessment of English grammar and mechanics. When introducing a new rule, a teacher can use one article as an instructional example and a second as an assessment of students' independent understanding. This book is an excellent tool for authentic assessment of knowledge of grammar and mechanics. The Scope and Sequence on page vii gives teachers an overview of the types of errors included in each article, enabling them to individualize lessons. Styles and Topics (p. x) lists the type of writing and the content for each exercise.

Suggested Uses for *Editor in Chief*®

Regular Usage

- Group instruction—EIC format is ideal for overhead projector.

- Cooperative Learning—Students edit and exchange work to proofread.

- Homework—Individual activities can follow class instruction.

Extension Activities

- Students write their own paragraphs for editing.

- EIC fosters class discussion of writing errors and how to avoid them.

- Checklist can be used to transfer editing skills to other writing activities.

Sources and Standards

In preparing this manuscript, we used the following references as standards for spelling, grammar, punctuation, and usage:

The American Heritage Dictionary, 3rd ed. (Boston: Houghton Mifflin Company, 1993).

The Chicago Manual of Style, 14th ed. (Chicago: The University of Chicago Press, 1993).

The Merriam-Webster Concise Handbook for Writers (Springfield, Mass.: Merriam-Webster Inc, 1991).

The Merriam-Webster Dictionary of English Usage (Springfield, Mass.: Merriam-Webster Inc, 1989).

The New York Public Library Writer's Guide to Style and Usage (New York: HarperCollins Publishers, Inc., 1994).

Warriner's English Grammar and Composition: Complete Course, Liberty Edition (Orlando: Harcourt Brace Jovanovich, 1986).

SCOPE AND SEQUENCE: *EDITOR IN CHIEF*® BOOK C2

TYPE OF ERROR	Exercise Number																																
	1	2	3	4	5	6	7	8	9	10	11	12	13	14	15	16	17	18	19	20	21	22	23	24	25	26	27	28	29	30	31	32	33
GRAMMAR/USAGE																																	
Adjective/adverb			■		■	■				■							■								■				■		■	■	
Agreement	■	■		■	■		■	■		■		■	■	■	■	■	■	■	■	■	■	■	■	■							■	■	
Article: a or an			■							■																					■		■
Conjunction: correlat.												■				■															■		■
Dangling modifier																	■							■	■	■	■						■
Misplaced modifier						■				■			■						■													■	
Nominative case								■																									
Parallel structure							■							■											■	■							
Pronoun: ambiguous							■					■				■			■		■								■	■	■		
Pronoun: with as/than			■									■						■															
Pronoun: subj./object		■	■					■												■		■				■			■	■		■	
Pronoun: reflexive												■																					
Subjunctive mood														■			■													■	■		
Tense: simple	■				■			■			■	■					■						■			■							
Tense: perfect	■	■						■	■				■						■	■	■						■	■					
Unnecessary words				■																													
Verbals									■								■												■				
Verb: infinitive		■	■			■				■			■							■													
Verb: participle			■	■						■			■						■	■													
Word pair (confused)			■	■	■	■	■		■	■	■	■	■	■		■						■		■	■	■	■	■	■		■		
SPELLING		■	■	■		■	■	■	■		■	■		■			■					■											
PUNCTUATION	1	2	3	4	5	6	7	8	9	10	11	12	13	14	15	16	17	18	19	20	21	22	23	24	25	26	27	28	29	30	31	32	33
Apostrophe	■	■		■	■		■	■	■	■	■	■					■		■			■				■	■		■	■		■	■
Colon	■			■													■				■			■			■		■	■	■		
Comma: absolute																												■					■
Comma: ambiguity											■		■																			■	■
Comma: appositive																■																	
Comma: conjunction																■			■		■							■					
Comma: contrast													■						■		■												
Comma: coord. adjec.							■				■						■														■		
Comma: date/address															■														■	■			
Comma: dialogue					■	■	■		■				■																				
Comma: interrupter		■																							■								
Comma: intro/transit.							■					■		■										■							■		
Comma: letter																					■												
Comma: nonessent.		■			■	■			■																■								■
Comma: quotation														■											■							■	
Comma: series														■		■	■								■							■	
Comma: splice						■							■			■									■	■							
Comma: unnecessary	■	■	■	■	■	■	■	■	■	■	■			■	■	■	■		■		■		■					■	■				
Exclamation point	■																		■														
Hyphen													■						■	■						■	■						
Multiple punctuation	■								■								■		■														
Parentheses					■																	■	■	■	■			■					
Period			■	■	■	■	■				■			■				■		■			■		■	■		■				■	■
Semicolon				■									■			■	■	■	■	■												■	■
Sentence fragment		■			■															■					■								
Question mark							■											■					■		■			■			■	■	■
Quotation marks									■		■	■	■																■	■		■	■
CAPITALIZATION	1	2	3	4	5	6	7	8	9	10	11	12	13	14	15	16	17	18	19	20	21	22	23	24	25	26	27	28	29	30	31	32	33
First word							■								■														■				
Compass direction																									■								
Proper noun/adjective			■		■	■			■					■			■			■			■	■	■								
Title/abbreviation														■	■		■												■	■	■		
Quotations						■																											
Seasons, holidays				■				■			■											■											

STYLES AND TOPICS: *EDITOR IN CHIEF®* BOOK C2

EXERCISE TITLE	WRITING STYLE	CONTENT: TOPIC	Fiction/ Nonfiction
1. Using Figurative Language	expository/descriptive	Comp./Lit.: figures of speech	nonfiction
2. Skeleton Crew	narrative	Fantasy: skeleton baseball	fiction
3. The Leopard Speaks	poem	Fantasy: animal	fiction
4. Keeping a Legend Alive	expository	Sports/History: marathon	nonfiction
5. Cross-Country Adventure	narrative	Adventure: skiing	fiction
6. A Capital Challenge	narrative	Adventure: scavenger hunt	fiction
7. Running for Fun and Fitness	expository	Fitness: running	nonfiction
8. Scheduling Conflict	narrative	Entertainment: TV programs	fiction
9. Enlightened about Electrons	dialog/expository	Science: electrons	fiction
10. Martian Canals Debunked	descriptive/expository	Science: astronomy	nonfiction
11. X Marks the Spot	narrative	Adventure: treasure hunt	fiction
12. Musical Tic-Tac-Toe	narrative	Music: game show	fiction
13. Easter Island Mystery	descriptive	Archaeology: Easter Island	nonfiction
14. Kindergarten Woes	narrative/analysis	Lit.: Hemingway story	fiction
15. A Questionable Bargain	persuasive (letter)	Economics: returning items	fiction
16. The Watergate Scandal	expository/timeline	History: Watergate/Nixon	nonfiction
17. Getting in Sync	narrative	Schedule: music classes	fiction
18. A Question of Gravity	narrative/expository	Science: gravity	fiction
19. Creatures That Glow in the Dark	expository/descriptive	Science: bioluminescence	fiction
20. E for Einstein	narrative	Biography: Einstein	fiction
21. Club Dread	descriptive (brochure)	Sports: sports club	fiction
22. To Sea by the Stars	descriptive	Science: celestial navigation	nonfiction
23. Campus Life	narrative (letter)	Education: college life	fiction
24. Gearing Up for Fun	descriptive/how-to	Game: directions	fiction
25. The Gypsy Life	expository	History/Culture: Gypsies	nonfiction
26. Waltzing into Trouble	narrative	Entertainment: dance	fiction
27. Supply and Demand	expository	Economics: supply/demand	nonfiction
28. An Alternative American Story	narrative/dialog	History: America	fiction
29. An A+ for C++	narrative/expository	Computers: programming	fiction
30. Biking Trail Debate	persuasive/dialog	Politics: local issue	fiction
31. A View to a Job	persuasive (letter)	Business: cover letter	fiction
32. Succeeding in Business	narrative/how-to	Economics: business tips	fiction
33. A Patent Lie?	narrative	Fantasy: alien encounter	fiction

Editor in Chief® — Editing Checklist

CAPITALIZATION

Are the correct words capitalized? Do other words need capitals?

CONTENT

Does the information in the paragraph match the caption and illustration?

GRAMMAR & USAGE

Agreement:

Does the verb agree with the subject? Is the subject collective? Does the pronoun agree with the noun or pronoun it replaces? Does the adjective agree with the noun or pronoun it modifies?

Correlative conjunctions:

Are either/or and neither/nor used correctly?

Dangling modifier:

Does the grammatical subject of the sentence immediately follow the introductory phrase, or does the sentence need to be rewritten?

Misplaced modifier:

Does the modifier make sense where it is placed within the sentence?

Parallel structure:

Are parallel ideas written in the same grammatical form within a sentence?

Pronoun:

Is it used as a subject or an object? Is the correct form used? Is it in the right place? Is it clear to which noun the pronoun refers?

Verbals:

Is the correct verb form used as a noun, adjective, or adverb?

Verb tense:

Is the correct form used for both helping verb and participle? Is the correct form used for both main verb and other verbs?

Usage:

Is the correct word used? Does a word need to be changed?

Word pairs that are easily confused:

Is the correct word used?

PUNCTUATION

Apostrophe:

Is the word a contraction? Is the word a plural or possessive? Is the apostrophe in the right place?

Colon:

Is it used correctly? Is it placed correctly?

Comma:

Is it needed to separate words, dates, phrases, or clauses? Is it placed correctly?

Exclamation point:

Is it used correctly?

Hyphen:

Is it used correctly in compound numbers or unit modifiers?

Question mark:

Is the sentence or quotation a question? Is the question mark placed correctly?

Quotation marks:

Is each part of the divided quotation enclosed? Are other punctuation marks placed correctly inside or outside the quotation marks? Are song, story, or chapter titles enclosed? Are single quotation marks required?

Run-on sentence:

Should this be more than one sentence? Should a period, a semicolon, or a conjunction be used?

Semicolon:

Is it needed? Is it used correctly?

Sentence fragment:

Is this a complete sentence?

SPELLING

Are the words spelled correctly? Is the plural form correct?

PROOFREADING

Should punctuation be inserted or deleted? Are there too many punctuation marks? Are parentheses used correctly in pairs? Are articles used correctly?

1. Using Figurative Language

If you have ever wrote a description, you may have used figures of speech known as similes and metaphors. These gems can improve anyones writing.

A simile or metaphor allow the reader to visualize more clearly who or what the author is describing. Using simile, the writer compares two unlike items directly, using the words *like* or *as* "He runs like the wind" or "The runner is as swift as the wind." The comparison in a metaphor is implied, and the writer states that one thing *is* another (though it is clearly not) "His heart is a stone." Either type of figurative language create a vivid image in the reader's mind.

Examples of simile and metaphor is found throughout literature. In his play *Romeo and Juliet*, Shakespeare wrote a metaphor comparing the young couples new love to a budding flower:

> This bud of love...,
> May prove a beauteous flower
>   when next we meet.

Herman Melville used this metaphor to describe the whale in his book *Moby Dick*:

> The glittering mouth yawned beneath the boat like an open-doored marble tomb.

It can be easy to overdo figurative language. Our daily speech is fill with

The quote above is an example of a simile, a figure of speech that uses either *like* or *as* to compare two unlike things. A metaphor is a figure of speech that compares two things without using *like* or *as*.

expressions used so often, that they have become cliches. Avoid writing such overused expressions as "neat as a pin" and "slept like a baby." It's also better not to mix figures of speech; the resulting images are often illogical "I'm keeping my eye on America's pulse, and I can feel the beat!"

The next time you write a story or a description, try using figurative language. It's "a piece of cake"

Find the 13 errors in this activity.
There are no errors in the illustration or the caption.

---

2. Skeleton Crew

On the night the museum paintings came alive, the skeletons from several paintings used the leg bones and hip bones to play baseball. Using the leg bones for bats and the kneecap bones for baseballs, they plaid for several hours in the main lobby, taking turns at bat.

In the room east of the lobby, other skeletons danced to the sounds of Boney Goodman and the Femurs. Some skeletons had to bone up on his steps but were back dancing soon.

In the room to the west of the lobby, still other skeletons practiced their card-playing skills with cards they had borrow from a painting full of dogs. One skeleton whom was a little rusty was told to found a different game. After one especially bonehead hand.

It was the baseball game, however, that was the most popular. Each side had the full team of five players, and the teams took turns pitching. Ground balls took sharp hops, when the bone bounced high off the wooden floor. Outfielders had trouble catching some line drives because they didn't have gloves. You had to really hand it to them for trying, though. Caution to be sure was a factor on some

These leg and kneecap bones from a museum painting look remarkably like baseballs and baseball bats. In fact, the skeletons from other paintings used them to play standard nine-player baseball on the night the paintings came alive.

plays. For instance, no one dared slide into a base for fear of going to pieces. Still, the skeletons enjoyed themselves immensely, playing into the we hours of the morning.

Finally, being game-weary and bone-tired, they set about their cleanup so that when the museum workers returned, they would see nothing amiss.

Find the 14 errors in this activity.
There are no errors in the illustration or the caption.

3. The Leopard Speaks

It's a honor to be chosen;
Yes, your Leopard King I'll be.
As judge I'll be most principaled
Uninterested as can be.

My background may be, like, spotty,
But, in fact, I have a nose
For sniffing out the fairest way
With which to have interposed.

From the very least noteworthy
To the more magnificent,
All cats will be respected—
No matter what they're scents.

Who is more equipped than me
The cat laws to create?
I'll carry them to other Cats
To who we all relate.

Enough you've had of business now;
Let's talk of racing games.
The members running furthest
Join the Leopards' Hall of Fame.

We shall lie out a giant feast,
When races have been run.
I will proclaim a holiday
Called day of leopard fun!

The English assignment was to write a poem from the animal's point of view. Rachonda imagined being chosen Leopard Queen; at left is the acceptance speech she wrote.

Find the 14 errors in this activity.
There are no errors in the illustration or the caption.

4. Keeping a Legend Alive

One of the favorite races of distance runners is the marathon. For some runners, the marathon is the ultimate test of endurance, for others, it's a stepping stone to even longer races. Some is 50 or even 100 miles long, but the principal yardstick by which all races are measured continues to be: the marathon.

The modern marathon began in the 1896 Olympics, held in Athens, and has been a part of the Olympics ever since. The event commemorates the legendary 25-mile run of Pheidippides northeast from Marathon to Athens to let the Athenians at home know of their warriors great victory over the Persians in 490 B.C. The Athenians, despite having 4,000 less soldiers than the invaders, halted the first large-scale Persian invasion of Greece.

Though the runner, Pheidippides, ran 25 miles, today's marathoners run 26.2 miles. The longer distance was first run at the 1908 Olympics in England (when the organizers wanted the race to start at Windsor Castle and finish in front of the royal box at the stadium in London and

In 490 B.C., an Athenian runner named Pheidippides ran the 25 miles from Marathon to Athens to announce the Athenian victory over invading Persian forces. In today's marathon, runners race 26.2 miles in commemoration of this legendary event.

was standardize at the 1924 Olympics in France.

Well-known United States marathon sites include New York, N.Y., Boston, Mass, and Big Sur, Calif.

Find the 13 errors in this activity.
There are no errors in the illustration or the caption.

---

5. Cross-Country Adventure

Andre heads into an unmarked area, drawn by the huge drifts of untouched powder. The previous nights storm has left almost a foot of fresh snow. As he slides along the base of the hill, he yells for the sheer joy of it, not knowing disaster is <u>eminent</u>. His echoing voice sets off a responding roar in the slope above him, and mountains of snow <u>come</u> tumbling down the hillside catching him like a huge wave. He rolls and tumbles down the slope, sinking deeper and deeper. Inside the snowy wave. His skis go flying, torn from his feet by the force of the avalanche.

When he stops moving, everything is still nothing is around him but the endless white; he is buried beneath the snow, his limbs <u>askew</u> from the impact. Can he move anything at all? Luckily, one arm lies close beside his head. He wriggles his fingers until he is able to clear a tiny air hole. He must be close to the surface, but the more he struggles, the more firmer he becomes wedged.

He now regrets having left the unmarked trail. He knows that he didn't tell anyone where he was going, and that there is little chance of another skier coming this way. How will anyone find him? He doesn't know how long he can remain buried this way; the wet snow is already beginning to soak through his clothes, and he is so cold, that his entire

Leaving the marked trail, Andre headed into the open woods, gleeful about all the new powder that had fallen overnight.

body throbs. "It's better than being numb, though," he thinks.

Either the cold or the lack of oxygen or both causes him to drift in and out of consciousness. Suddenly, hands reach down into the snow, grab him, and pull him up. He gasps for air as he reaches the surface.

The rescue team is relieved that they have found him in time. A snowmobiler who ventured into the same area had found Andre's skis sticking out of the snow and alerted the ski patrol, "I'm glad to be alive," Andre tells his Dad. "I will never take Mother Nature for granted again Pop."

Find the 14 errors in this activity.
There are no errors in the illustration or the caption.

6. A Capital Challenge

"To find the first of six destinations, start at the building that honors are first president" the instructions read. Leroy went to the Washington Monument. "Climb the steps, and stop at the seventy-sixth step. Pickup the piece of paper taped to the handrail, and climb back down. Hold the piece of paper up to a mirror to see where to go next"

Holding the paper up to a mirror, Leroy saw the words "War" and "Wall," so he went to the Vietnam Veterans Memorial. It took a few minutes to walked the long way along the wall, and he saw on their faces many people studying the names on the wall with faraway looks. Under the rock, at the end of the long list of names, was his last set of instructions. "find the second mirror, go to what you see reflected, and read the words of a famous speech. Return to where you started, and say the first six words of the speech. You're done."

This last clue was a real tough one, but Leroy finally figured out that the second mirror was the Reflecting Pool and that what he saw in it was the reflection of the

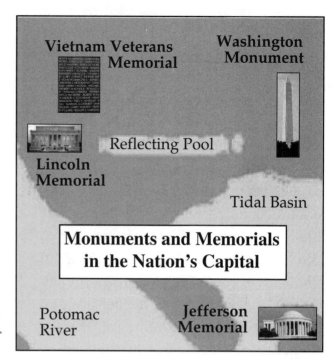

Leroy found the Washington, D.C., scavenger hunt challenging, but rewarding. He visited four monuments and memorials in the process.

Lincoln Memorial. He went to the Memorial and read the gettysburg address which is carved into rock many feet high. He took the most direct route, over the Potomac River, to his first destination and recited the first six words of Lincoln's speech: "Four score and seven years ago." Leroy had finished the scavenger hunt.

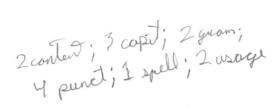

Find the 14 errors in this activity.
There are no errors in the illustration or the caption.

7. Running for Fun and Fitness

Running is a good way to improve your overall fitness; the affects of such exercise can be dramatic, offering benefits to your muscles, your blood flow, and how you think.

To start with, running increases the anaerobic capacity of your lungs. That is, you can breathe in more air each time you inhale. This makes your heart stronger and also increases the flow of oxygen though your bloodstream, helping flush harmful, unwanted bacteria; and chemicals out of your system.

Running also helps you burn fat. The thing to remember, though, is that the faster you run, the more carbohydrates you burn. To take off the fat, you need to run more slowly and for a longer period of time. Your body should be able to sustain a longer run if it's a slower run. The question is, how slowly should you run? The key is to keep moving. Even if you think you're going too slowly, you're still getting the cardiovascular benefits that running provides.

Running can help you escape the demands of everyday living, enabling you to think of things, other than a job or

Running can be a good source of physical and mental fitness for people of all ages and abilities. One of the benefits is an increased aerobic capacity, which is the ability of the lungs to take in more oxygen with each breath.

school. Running can also clear your head and offer you a new way to look at a situation. As a result, both body and mind gets a workout.

Running can be good for your health and is also an enjoyable way to spend time. As someone once said "Time flies when you're having fun running."

Find the 14 errors in this activity.
There are no errors in the illustration or the caption.

8. Scheduling Conflict

Diane had a big-time problem on her hands; one of her stars was leaving.

Diane was head of programming for FAVE-TV, and she needed a Fall replacement for Michael Baker, whom was leaving the highly rated "True Crime" series for a career in movies. Everybody else in the management circle was holding their breath, but it looked like Baker was on his way out.

One option, of course, was to continue the show with a new host. However, Baker had become immensely popular in certain big-city markets. It was him who had convinced many people to watch the low-rated "On the Police Beat," at 9 o clock, just so they could be right on time for "True Crime" at 10 and would'nt have to leave "Movie of the Week" or "Thad's Science Fiction Theater" halfway through. Advertisers had pick up on this trend and started paying for time during "On the Police Beat," so the show stayed on the air. Baker was the real draw, and it was an open secret to whomever was in the know.

None of the network's four half-hour shows, which aired from 8 to 10 P.M., were top-rated shows, although, they were all near the top. What could compete with "I Love Lucido?" It was "True Crime" that was the real moneymaker for the

SUNDAY NIGHT PROGRAMMING			
	WAVE-TV	**CAVE-TV**	**FAVE-TV**	**DAVE-TV**

	WAVE-TV	CAVE-TV	FAVE-TV	DAVE-TV
7:00	I Love Lucido	Miss Michelle	Carrie Goes to the Zoo	History Comes Alive
7:30	Pauline on the Scene	Not Another Dear John	Cheryl's Undersea Camera	
8:00	Foster's Corner	Movie of the Week	Hockett's Healthy Living	True Mysteries of Science
8:30	Hanson and Co.		Linda's Slice of Life	
9:00	Mystery Movie with Carole Bannes		On the Police Beat	Thad's Science Fiction Theater
9:30				
10:00		Local News	True Crime with Michael Baker	
10:30		Lockwood Live!		

This schedule lists the television shows that the four major networks offer every Sunday night.

relatively new FAVE-TV, which begun as a regional network just 10 years ago.

The top brass had offered Baker alot more money, reportedly double his salary, but he hadn't budged. He already had creative control of the show, which had whetted his appetite for directing big-budget motion pictures. He also knew he will be able to command a higher salary in the movie industry.

The programming directors at the other three major networks were smiling, but for Diane the question remained, "Where was the next Michael Baker?"

Find the 15 errors in this activity.
There are no errors in the illustration or the caption.

---

9. Enlightened about Electrons

"What's the big deal about those particles?" Yebio asked his oldest brother, Dan. "The pictures I've saw show electrons as tiny, black balls travelling around the nucleus of an atom as marbles. How exciting can that be?"

"Electrons do more than act like particles," Dan replied. "Scientists have found that electrons sometimes act like waves! Imagine vibrations of energy like clouds around the nuculus."

"Okay, I can except that," said Yebio "but what did an atom ever do for me?"

"Well, if it weren't for atoms, you couldn't see," he said, "because light is created by the processes within the atom."

Yebio was starting to get interest.ed "What does an atom have to do give off light?"

Dan thought for a moment. "I'll give you a clue. Electrons are at different energy levels as they change relationship to the nucleus. When an electron moves from lower energy to higher energy, light is absorbed. In other words, as it moves outward from the nucleus, the electron gains energy."

Yebio digested the information and replied, "Then I guess light must be given

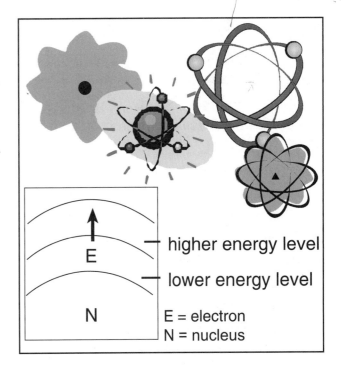

As shown at the top of the illustration, atoms can be represented in a variety of ways. We can think of electrons as particles of matter orbiting the nucleus of an atom or as clouds of energy. Light is absorbed as the electron climbs to a higher energy level, away from the nucleus (shown at bottom of illustration).

off when an electron moves away from the nucleus."

"Exactly! An electron moving to a position of lower energy releases light."

Yebio was fully intrieged with the concept. "Well, from my position," he retorted, "I'm beginning to 'see the light!'"

Find the 15 errors in this activity.
There are no errors in the illustration or the caption.

10. Martian Canals Debunked

Before people could plain see that the surface of Mars was desolate and rocky, popular belief held that the Red Planet could once have been inhibited by people very much as us.

In the late 1870's, the Italian Astronomer Giovanni Schiaparelli started the controversy by announcing on the surface of Mars that he had observed what he thought were faint lines. He called these faint lines *canali*, which English translators mistakenly took to means canals. Because canals occur naturally and channels are manmade, evidence of canals on Mars would suggest a advanced civilization.

American astronomer Percival Lowell popularized this belief in Martian canals in the early part of the 20th century by claiming to have affective evidence of the presence of underground canals on Mars. Indeed, Lowell published three books trying to convince others of the existence of canals only when astronomers had telescopes powerful enough to prove that the "canals" were really channels, did the *canali* clamor subside. Nevertheless, the debate over life on Mars rage on.

This drawing, based on what some astronomers thought they saw, suggests the existence of canals on Mars. Since canals are manmade (whereas channels occur naturally), many people believed drawings like this to be evidence of civilization on Mars.

Find the 14 errors in this activity.
There are no errors in the illustration or the caption.

11. X Marks the Spot

Fred clambered along the steep rocky hillside slipping and sliding in the mud. Torrential rains from winter's angry outburst had loosened the soil, and mudslides had altered the banks above the river. The *X* indicated an area below where the river forked, but it was impossible to pinpoint exactly where along the western fork of the river this spot was. Suddenly the ground gave way. He grabbed a nearby fern to keep from falling, but succeeded only in uprooting the plant as he fell. He slid and rolled down the steep slope, landing at the base of the hill.

As he struggled to his feet, muddied and bruised, he notices an opening among two large rocks. He pulled out his flashlight and peered closer. A sudden glimmer caught his eye. He put the flashlight back on his belt and pulled away rocks and debris from the opening until he was able to wedge himself through. He found him in what seemed to be a cave. As his eyes adjusted to the darkness, he felt around for his flashlight, which had fallen from his belt. He quickly found it. As he picked it up, his fingers brushed against something hard, cold, and distinctly bony—something dead.

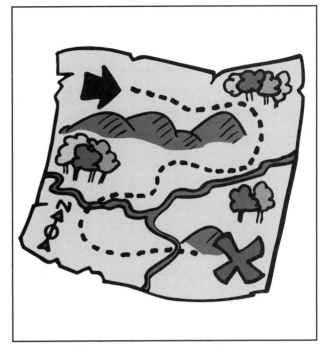

While on vacation in the Caribbean, Fred Holtz made a "bone-afide" discovery when he decided to follow the trail shown on an old treasure map he had found at the bottom of an antique chest!

Swinging it around, he saw the golden light that had previously caught his eye. Propped against the wall was a cobweb-covered skeleton, and around it's neck, hanged a golden medallion. The medallion looked just like one he had seen in a painting of the infamous pirate, Varnet. Had he discovered the last resting place of this notorious brigand? "Well, yo ho ho," he sang, and a bag full of gold. I'll be rich!" Could anyone be as lucky as him?

Find the 16 errors in this activity.
There are no errors in the illustration or the caption.

---

12. Musical Tic-Tac-Toe

"Welcome to Musical Tic-Tac-Toe. Todays theme is composers. Behind each treble clef is a picture of a composer. Each time a player chooses a square, they are flipped. A correct identification gains the player an outlined picture an incorrect answer means the picture is flipped back over. Get any three in a row to win.

"Let's get to it. Player One, you've chosen to start in the center. Here's your clue: This German composer wrote nine symphonys, but the first four notes of his Symphony No. 5 are possibly the most recognized in the world. Who is he?"

"He is Beethoven."

"Ludwig van Beethoven is correct. The center picture is now outlined in black. Player Two chooses the top left square. This Austrian composer wrote more than 100 symphonies and was referred to even by his contemporaries as 'Papa'."

"That would be Haydn."

"Franz Joseph Haydn is correct. Your picture is outlined in gray, and you've blocked your opponent. Player One wants the top middle square. This American become known as the father of ragtime."

"I'll say Joplin."

"Scott Joplin is correct. Player Two has now chosen the bottom middle square. This German's works both include operas and orchestral pieces, but he is most famous for his oratorio *Messiah*."

"Is it Chopin?"

"Correct. You've got another block. Yes,

The composers in the gameboard, from left to right, are as follows: top, Franz Joseph Haydn, Scott Joplin, and Wolfgang Amadeus Mozart; middle, Ludwig van Beethoven; and bottom, Giuseppe Verdi and George Frederic Handel. Photos are outlined in black or white according to which player answered a question correctly.

Player One, you can have the top right square. This Austrian started composing at age five. He is famous for the opera *The Magic Flute*. Who is he"?

"He is Mozart."

"Wolfgang Amadeus Mozart is correct. Player Two, which space would you like? To the bottom right we go. This Italian composer is famous for his operas, including *Rigoletto* and *Aida*. Who is he?"

"I'd say it's Puccini."

"No. Player One do you know?"

"Yes. It's Verdi."

"Giuseppe Verdi is right. You've won!"

Find the 14 errors in this activity.
There are no errors in the illustration or the caption.

---

13. Easter Island Mystery

On Easter of 1722, a Dutch admiral named Jacob Roggeveen discovered the small polynesian island he later named Easter Island. Nearing the shore, admiral Roggeveen was astounded to see huge stone figures on raised platforms with long ears.

The island was peopled by two distinct groups: those who had long ears (stretched to hold wooden plugs) and regular-eared people. With this revelation, visitors to the island was able to imply that the statues had been made by the long eared people.

There has been much conjecture about the method used to raise these huge monuments from their prone positions. The islanders had no heavy wood with which to create lifting equipment, yet they had able to erect hard-lava sculptures weighing up to 50 tons and standing as tall as 40 feet. In 1956, Thor Heyerdahl, Norwegian archaeologist, enlisted twelve island men to show how the objects could have been lifted. Though it took 18 days the men raised a 20-ton statue from where it lied using only muscles, poles, and stones.

An even bigger mystery has been the means of transporting statues from the quarry to the display platforms. Asked to reveal the secret, islanders insisted that the statues had walked under their own power not by someone elses! Some

Above are pictures of Easter Island statues in rough hewn (left) and final stages (right). Made to honor the dead, they were displayed on funeral platforms called "ahus." The statues weigh up to 100,000 pounds each and are 12 to 30 feet high.

researchers, however, came up with the explanation that the statues could of been rocked, side to side, while being pulled by rope (similar to the way in which we might move an upright refrigerator). The affect would have been that the statues appeared, from a distance, to be walking!

However these unusual statues came to stand guard on Easter Island, they provide a tantalizing mystery to students, researchers, and other inquiring minds.

Find the 16 errors in this activity.
There are no errors in the illustration or the caption.

---

14. Kindergarten Woes

Alan pondered for a moment before beginning his analysis. He would have to write speedily in order to finish.

In Ernest Hemingway's short story "A Clean, Well-Lighted place", the character of the old man is seen through the eyes of two men whom Hemingway simply chooses to call "the older waiter" and "the younger waiter." A contrast is established not only between youth and old age but also between the empathy of the younger waiter and the intolerance of the older waiter. The younger waiter sees nothing but a nasty old man which is keeping him from his wife and home. To the younger waiter, the old man is just another drunk who should move on. An impression that is made clear when he complains to the older waiter, "Hombre, there are bodegas open all night long." The younger waiter does not understand what it is like to be alone in the world. He has youth, a family to go home to, a future, and hope. He boasts, "I am confidence. I am all confidence". The older waiter, however, sees a very different man. He sees a clean man who drinks without spilling. He sees a man who once had a wife: a man who, like himself, needs the semblance of normalcy that he finds in the clean, well-lighted cafe, the cafe, unlike the bodega, is a place where decency and order can be found.

"Boys and girls," Mrs. Crabtree interrupted, snack time is over. find your

Child prodigy Alan Allredynoes spent his snack time proofing his latest analysis of Hemingway's "A Clean, Well-Lighted Place." He wanted to establish a contrast between the older, more understanding waiter and the younger, insensitive waiter.

places on the floor, and cross your hands, and legs."

"If only I was a little older," Alan sighed, "I could rid myself of these silly little snack breaks. When will I ever finish this analyses! Did Poe or Einstein have to stop when snack break ended or sit with his hands and legs crossed?! The injustices of kindergarten is vast."

Find the 15 errors in this activity.
There are no errors in the illustration or the caption.

15. A Questionable Bargain

1662 Camino Sierra
Bakersfield CA 93306
March 11, 1999

Danson's Deals (D.D.)
Customer Service Department
P.O. Box 11196
Houston, TX 77111

To whom it may concern,

Enclosed you will find several items that I am returning; one pair of clogs, $37, one skirt, $29, a child's dress and hat, $15, and a child's T-shirt, $9. On February 19, 1999 I spoke to Madeline Gonzales Director of Customer Service at D.D.'s main office in Tulsa, Okla. She told me that, although I did not have a receipt, I could return the items. If there were manufacturer's defects or other problems.

At the time I made the purchase, I thought the deals were "too good to be true;" after receiving the items, I realized I was right. The skirt was missing a button, the T-shirt turned an entire load of wash pink, and the dress and matching hat was stained. In addition, the clogs were two different sizes: neither were the size six, that I ordered.

Shown above are the items Mei Lee purchased. With the eight percent sales tax, her order came to nearly one hundred dollars.

Either I would like a complete refund of my money or store credit for the total (price + tax = $96.30.) Included in the envelope is my account number and credit card number.

I look forward to your prompt reply.

Sincerely

Mei Lee
Mei Lee

Find the 16 errors in this activity.
There are no errors in the illustration or the caption.

16. The Watergate Scandal

The Watergate investigation uncovered one of the biggest political scandals in United States history.

In June, 1972, five men hired by the Republican Party's Committee for the Re-election of the President (C.R.P.) were arrested for breaking into the Democratic Party's national headquarters. The men were charged with several crimes, including: burglary and wiretapping. President Richard Nixon immediately directed White House Counsel John Dean to begin a coverup. Accusations that any White House official had been involved, were repeatedly denied, although reports to the contrary were soon uncovered by the media.

The Senate Select Committee on Presidential Campaign Activities were organized to investigate the affair in February 1973. Shortly after that, Nixon accepted the resignations of several of his Advisors (including John Dean) however, Nixon continued to deny it.

In May 1973, the committee began hearings on the Watergate matter. John Dean accused the President of a coverup. Three months later, the committee learned that Nixon had in his office a recording system, that he had used to tape conversations. Select tapes were promptly subpoenaed but Nixon refused to turn them over, claiming it was his executive

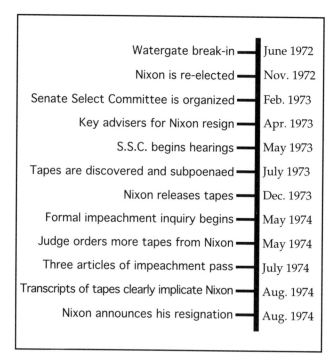

Watergate break-in	June 1972
Nixon is re-elected	Nov. 1972
Senate Select Committee is organized	Feb. 1973
Key advisers for Nixon resign	Apr. 1973
S.S.C. begins hearings	May 1973
Tapes are discovered and subpoenaed	July 1973
Nixon releases tapes	Dec. 1973
Formal impeachment inquiry begins	May 1974
Judge orders more tapes from Nixon	May 1974
Three articles of impeachment pass	July 1974
Transcripts of tapes clearly implicate Nixon	Aug. 1974
Nixon announces his resignation	Aug. 1974

The timeline of events shown above details the Watergate scandal. The coverup began six days after the break-in.

privilege to keep the tapes. The Supreme Court voted unanimously that the tapes were not covered by executive privilege, eight hours after the judgment, Nixon released the tapes.

A formal impeachment inquiry began in May 1973. Two months later, the House Judiciary Committee recommended four articles of impeachment. In August, Nixon released additional transcripts of tapes, that clearly implicated him in the coverup and with his credibility badly damaged in Congress, Nixon announced his resignation and became the first President of the United States to resign from office.

Find the 15 errors in this activity.
There are no errors in the illustration or the caption.

17. Getting in Sync

Jogging past the womens' dormitory of her new college, Melody Horn was feeling "jazzed;" she fell into a rhythm with another runner who didn't seem as anxious to start school.

"If I would only have learned to schedule my time during the first year," Ann Holtzmann complained, "I will have gotten some Bs and maybe an A or two. I wouldn't have fallen flat!"

"You can't beat time management. They really drummed it in at my high school—my whole class improved its grades. Now, though, I have to pick my classes and learn to study in a new place. These kind of responsibilities are tough."

"You sound pretty sharp," Ann noted. "What do you want to do here?"

"I have a natural inclination for music, so I'll study that as my major. I need Music Theory I, and I must choose among the other two music classes offered to freshmen. I just hope I get flexible teachers."

"Not all the staff is the same, so don't leave it to chance. If I was you, I'd take Sak for Music Theory I. Make a note of it!"

"Oh, no! Taking Sak would mean a Friday class. Well, that's a minor concern if she's well at teaching. Anyway, given up Ono's section one will free me to take the section three techniques class from Oz.

CLASS	SEC	TIME	INST
Music Theory I	1	MW 9–11	Ono
	2	TTh 2–4	Ono
	3	Sat 8–12	Sak
Rhythm Patterns	1	MWF 1–2	Vert
	2	TTh 3–4:30	Vert
Improvisation Techniques	1	TW 1–4	Oz
	2	MF 2–5	Oz
	3	WF 9–12	Gold

Melody would choose all her first-semester music classes from the mini-schedule shown above.

Let's see, for general education I'll take an English writing course and a History class. Algebra or a general math class are required, so I'm hoping to take the Math for Musicians class. I'll schedule my assignment and practice times around all my classes."

"By the time you start second semester, you will already take most of your freshman requirements! I think I'll sign up for time management!" Ann yelled, heading for the locker room.

Melody continued her run solo, glad that Ann was singing a new tune.

Find the 18 errors in this activity.
There are no errors in the illustration or the caption.

18. A Question of Gravity

"Aristotle, famed scientist and philosopher, argued that heavy objects fall faster than light objects. Mathematician, astronomer, and physicist, Galileo, stated that light and heavy objects fall at the same rate. Who was right? Today, I will test these theories and let you, my fellow classmates, see who's theory is correct."

"I have in my hands two objects: a hardball and a pingpong ball. If dropped at the same time, how many of you think the hardball will hit the floor first?" Jarrod asked his captive audience. "How many of you think the balls will hit at the same time?" Jarrod recorded the results on the chalkboard, alot more students agreed with Aristotle. "I will now drop both objects at the same time and from the same height. I want you to closely watch"! Jarrod dropped the objects. As the majority of the class had anticipated, the balls hit the ground at different times. "Very good, you've been as studious as me. Alright, I have one more experiment to perform. This should be a piece of cake for smart students like ourselves."

Jarrod pulled out two pieces of paper from his binder and crumpled one of them up. "How many of you think these two pieces of paper will hit at the same time?". A few students agreed that both pieces of paper would hit at the same time. Several more were undecided. "I am holding both papers at the same height, and I am now

Using a pingpong ball and a hardball in the first part of his demonstration, Jarrod proved that objects of differing weights fall at the same rate.

dropping it at the same time." The crumpled paper landed first. "I ask you now Was Galileo right only some of the time? Is gravity not constant?" Jarrod paused momentarily. "Yes, gravity is constant! What you have witnessed here is air resistance. The flat unaltered sheet has more air resistance than the crumpled sheet of paper, so it falls more slowly. Galileo's law of falling objects, therefore, can be proven only when there is no air resistance."

The class applauded. Jarrod's demonstration was sure to recieve high marks.

Find the 18 errors in this activity.
There are no errors in the illustration or the caption.

---

19. Creatures that Glow in the Dark

Bioluminescence, the emission of light produced by some living organisms, is a fascinating if little-known subject. Fireflies are the most common example of terrestrial animals that glow in the dark but the majority of luminous organisms are marine animals. That lived in moderate to great depths.

Bioluminescence involves light production without heat. Either an animal can be self-luminescent producing its own light, or they may use the light from parasitic bacteria carried in its body in gland-like structures. Most animals that glow are self-luminescent, producing light by a chemical reaction. The enzyme luciferase promotes a reaction, between oxygen and a substance in the organism called luciferin. It usually takes place in special organs called photophores. The pattern and the amount of light can vary.

Scientists are still hypothesizing about the reasons why animals produce light? Sexual attraction may be one reason; the fireflies flashing abdomens attract mates. The opposing roles of predator and prey offer further possible reasons for animal bioluminescence. Some animals use light as a lure for attracting prey, for example, the aptly named anglerfish has a photophore (a bulblike light organ) at the base of a long, flexible rod that it can dangle in front of its mouth like a fishing line with bait. Other fish use their light displays to avoid becoming prey, using flashing light patterns while they escape

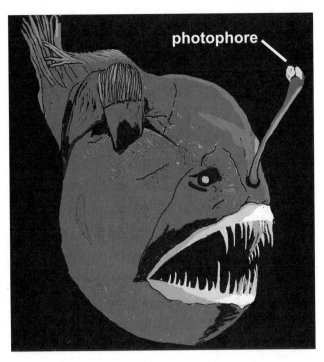

photophore

There are two types of light organs (photophores) in bioluminescent animals. Self-luminescent animals with true photophores produce their own light chemically; other animals carry symbiotic light-producing bacteria in their bodies. The anglerfish, pictured above, has a flexible rod with an organ that contains luminescent bacteria. It uses this rod to attract prey.

to distract their predators. The Atlantic midshipman is a fish known to flash its light on, and off at approaching predators, perhaps warning them away from its venomous spine. Another way to avoid enemies is by counterillumination. The fish matches the intensity and angle of sunlight with its own luminescence, thereby erasing its shadow.

Scientists still have a great deal to learn about bioluminescence. As exploration into the deep sea increases, they would be able to learn even more about how and why so many marine animals glow in the dark.

Find the 16 errors in this activity.
There are no errors in the illustration or the caption.

---

20. *E* for Einstein

Many of us know Albert Einstein for his equation, E = nc² and the idea that energy is simply mass that is "frozen". Each of us who has heard of Albert Einstein and his theories has their image of Albert the genius. However, what do we know of Albert, the child who became the famous man?

Albert was seen as an unpromising youth for several reasons (in fact, his success would surprise many people:) his early slowness in learning, his disdain for physical activity, and his dislike of school. Albert did not learn to speak until he was three years old (not by the usual age two!) He did not enjoy outdoor childrens' games; he complained that strenuous, physical activity made him dizzy. Instead he would spend his time playing games in solitude. Because of his disdain for a coercive teaching style, Albert was often unpopular with teachers. His Greek teacher was so unimpressed with Albert's scholarship, that he said Albert would fail at any occupation he undertook.

Despite the unfavorable reports, there was also clues to Albert's potential: his musical interest and ability, his self-taught mastery of geometry and calculus, and his intense interest in how the world worked. Given a compass, young Albert

Though he worked on many equations, Einstein is most famous for the one above, in which *E* stands for energy, *m* for mass, and *c* for the speed of light. The equation implies that mass is a solid form of energy.

found that the needle always pointed in the same direction. He was impressed by the mysterious behavior of such devices, and set out to learn more. He felt that behind worldly objects there was something "deeply hidden:" the inner miracles that make up the outer world.

For good or bad, Albert Einstein's early years' have contributed to a mystique that has never wore off. Who knows in what child the next genius lurks?

Find the 17 errors in this activity.
There are no errors in the illustration or the caption.

---

21. Club Dread

Do you have a

notion for motion, a
need for speed, or a
yearn for the burn?

If you answered "Yes"! and have passed a rigerous physical exam, come test your metal. (Warning: this resort is for the intrepid-action addict not for the faint of heart!)

We offer a wide variety of action-packed sports, including zesty winter challenges (cool)! and sizzling summer adventures (hot!). See details on page 4. (Note that waterskiing and snow skiing is offered seasonally only.)

Read what customers, Do, Chang, and Folly, have to say about are resort:

"The club fits my needs 'to a tee."
"It gives Bob and I the biggest thrill!"
"This is definitely not for 'wimps'."

By the time you leave, you will have confronted your fears, rose to their challenge, and conquered those fears!

Seventeen-year-old Jo Muletti learned that Club Dread had hundreds of satisfied customers and that it offered all the sports pictured above year-round. She made sure she met the physical requirements and then completed the application (results are reflected in brochure shown).

Please give all information indicated.

Emergency contact:

Name: Jo Muletti

Martha Turner, (206) 555-8893

Phone: (206) 555-0029

Do you meet physical criterions?

Age: 18

E-mail Address: jmulet@abc.net

Will you sign a release form? Yes

Find the 17 errors in this activity.
There are no errors in the illustration or the caption.

22. To Sea by the Stars

For centuries, sailors have measured their ships' positions at sea by observing the Sun, Moon planets, and stars. Measuring latitude was relatively easy, since it was based on the altitude of the Sun above the horizon. However, it wasn't until the 18th century that sailors were able to devise a method for determining longitude. Called "celestial navigation", this is based on the idea that a heavenly body is directly over a specific point on the earth's surface at a giving time. By observing the direction of a star from the ship and measuring its angle above the horizon, the navigator can ascertain how far the ship is from the earthly position of the star. Earthly position indicates where a heavenly body would be, if it were to drop at an angle to the earth.

To find the exact position of the ship, the navigator picks three stars. Using a sextant (an instrument developed in the mid-1800s), the navigator measures the angle that each make with the horizon. The angle of each star and the time it was measured is recorded.

The navigator then consults an Almanac, which lists the predicted, earthly positions of selective heavenly bodies based on their angles at specific times and dates, and plots these positions

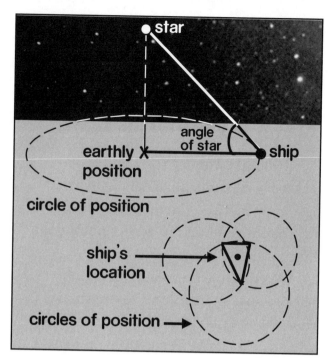

Sailors have long used the positions of stars and other heavenly bodies to find their way at sea. In the mid-18th century, an instrument called the sextant was devised for determining longitude at sea based on the earthly positions of certain stars.

on a map of the area. The earthly position is the center of an imaginary circle called a "circle of position." Because the circles are so large, the navigator usually draws only a portion of each indicating where the circles overlap (as shown in the illustration.) This intersection of the three lines forms a triangle, the ship's position is at the approximate center of this triangle.

Find the 15 errors in this activity.
There are no errors in the illustration or the caption.

---

23. Campus Life

852 College Blvd.
Dormitory A-4
Los Angeles, CA 90001
September 1, 1999

Dear Rochelle

I have finally arrived at the University of California. It is much different from life in the south and Junior college! Luckily, I got a campus tour before classes started.

Right now, I'm in the middle of tryouts for the women's dance team. The team all works very hard together to get the best new members. I hope my cheerleading experience and eleven years of dancing gives me an edge on the competition. At this point, though, it's anyone's guess as to who will make the team.

I'd also like to sign up for the business club here on campus, although I might have missed the new member deadline. A few of the people who live in my dormitory is part of the club and say it's one of the most prestigious business clubs around. If I would have known about it sooner, I'd have made it to the first meeting. (Who would have thought sign-ups were the week before classes?)

My roommate and me are getting along well. If we were a little less busy, we'd have more time to just hang out." She's taking 19 units! (Last semester, she made

It was 6:00 P.M. when Natalie concluded the letter to her friend Rochelle, who lives in Little Rock, Arkansas. She would have to rush to make it to dance tryouts on time.

straight As with 17 units)! Can you imagine anyone taking such a heavy load. I wonder how she does it?

I must go now, Rochelle. The dance team meets in 15 minutes! I'm sure by the time I have a chance to write to you again, the Fall semester already will have flew by. Take care of yourself, and write back soon.

Love

Natalie

Find the 18 errors in this activity.
There are no errors in the illustration or the caption.

---

24. Gearing Up for Fun

Directions for Playing "In Gear"
(2–4 players)

Object:

Move all six of your peg from Start to Finish. This must be done by turning a gears so that pegs from one gear lined up with a hole in the next gear.

Method—

1. Place a peg in the Start hole at the beginning of a turn. (The Start hole is the one to which the stationery arrow points.)

2. Shake, and throw the dice to get the number of moves allowed for the turn. Pegs are moved by turning the gears in which they ride. (Remember this: when you move one gear, both gears move!) One move equals 1/12 revolution of the gear. (Each hole moves to the position of an adjacent hole).

3. Turn both gears by pushing the first gear at Start (you may push it either clockwise or counterclockwise) to get your peg as close as possible to the second gear. You may not accede the number of allowed moves. An example follows:

   If you threw an "8", you could get your Start peg to line up with the second gear by turning the first gear

Melissa rolled an "8." She has already moved the first gear counterclockwise and can now jump her Start peg to the second gear. She will move the gears by two teeth to get her other peg to the Finish hole. She will use her final moves to advance her remaining peg by two teeth.

clockwise by four teeth. After transferring a peg you would still have four moves left (eight minus four;) therefore, you could turn the gear until your peg was one tooth from Finish

4. Continue to play following the rules until all your pegs have reach Finish. The first player too reach this goal wins!

Find the 16 errors in this activity.
There are no errors in the illustration or the caption.

---

25. The Gypsy Life

Gypsies have long been a subject of interest to many people. Their nomadic lifestyle and professions fortune telling and animal tamer, for example) have created an image of the exotic Gypsy.

The nomadic Gypsies travel seasonal along specific routes that connect him to other bands of Gypsies. Their migratory nature has taken them from their origins in India to northern Europe in the eleventh century, to southwestern Europe in the fourteenth century, and to western Europe in the fifteenth century and the second half of the twentieth century has seen Gypsies spread throughout north and South America and Asia. Estimating their population has been almost impossible because of their extensive and constant travel. At present, there may be as little as one million or as many as six million.

Traditionally, Gypsies have pursued occupations that make it easy to travel. Men were metalsmiths, musicians, livestock traders, and animal trainers and exhibitors. Women were most common fortune tellers, beggars, entertainers, and potion sellers.

Today, industrialism and growing urban influences are changing the

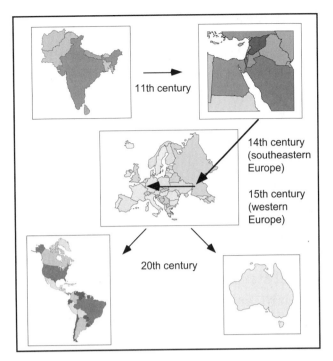

From their origin in India, Gypsies spread to the Middle East and then to Europe. Today, Gypsies can be found in the Americas and Australia as well.

traditional Gypsy ways. Instead of doing metal work, mechanics is now a common occupation for Gypsies. Their modes of transportation has shifted from riding horses and walking to driving cars and flying. Now, there are reports that even traveling is declining. How the future effect Gypsy culture remains to be seen. Is the Gypsy culture on the brink of extinction or simply in the process of evolution?

Find the 15 errors in this activity.
There are no errors in the illustration or the caption.

26. Waltzing into Trouble

I had scarcely never been so embarrassed in my life as I was at the mayor's ball!

My friend, Greg, and I had been taking lessons in ballroom dance for several months, and we just had to show off our new skills to the revered attendees. The viennese waltz can be difficult to execute, but we thought we would navigate the floor with no problem.

All started well. With the downbeat, we commenced our ill fated swirling tour, weaving between and around other dancers. (We even turned up our noses at other dancer's steps.) My steps were well placed when I crossed my feet for the turns, my dance form was implacable.

A couple moving into our path caused a real turn of events. To avoid them, Greg turned us in a new direction. Momentarily distracted, my next step was faulty, one heel catching in my other shoe. The floor seemed to fly up at us before I knew what has happened! Some of the other dancers barely avoided spilling on top of us, while others struggled to suppressing there laughter. I just wished the floor would open up and swallow ourselves.

Melanie and Greg finished the waltz with elegance. Only seconds earlier, they were sprawled in a mass on the floor, scarlet dress tangled in arms and legs. Though their faces remained nearly the color of Melanie's dress, they survived the remaining two minutes of the waltz without mishap.

Despite the fiasco, we remembered Instructor Kims motto that "the show must go on", and we got up. We dusted us off, and pretended that we couldn't careless about falling. We put the best face on a bad situation by finishing in style without showing any embarrassment.

Find the 18 errors in this activity.
There are no errors in the illustration or the caption.

27. Supply and Demand

Two of the most basic concepts of economics are supply and demand. Supply is how much is available, and demand is how much people are wanting. These concepts can be applied to almost any good or service.

For example, the supply of bread will raise if it's in demand because sellers know that people will buy them. However, the supply of bread will fall if people no longer want to buy it (a decrease in it's demand) because sellers won't maintain a supply of something they can't sell.

Often shown as curves on graphs, economists make a habit of tracking supply and demand. Supply increases as demand decreases, the opposite is also true. On a graph, these curves would meet at some point. This intersection is called: the equilibrium level because it is the level of highest satisfaction for both buyer and seller. Excluding other factors the equilibrium level will result in supply matching demand.

One thing often tracked on a supply-demand Graph is price. For example, supply can be shown as the number of loaves of bread offered on grocery store shelves each week, and demand can be shown as the price paid for each loaf of bread. According to the graph (which

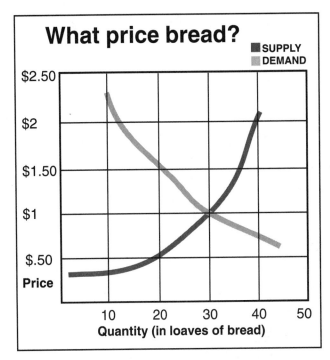

This supply-demand graph shows the relationship between number of loaves of bread offered and price paid for each loaf. The equilibrium price, which makes both consumers and producers happy, is where the supply and demand curves meet.

shows that 15 loafs would be bought at a price of $2.25) the equilibrium price for 30 loaves of bread is $1.25 each.

In the real world though the graph is just a model. Experience drives today's economic markets more than any economist manufactured model. Still, supply and demand are powerful phenomenon that every buyer and seller should consider.

Find the 16 errors in this activity.
There are no errors in the illustration or the caption.

---

28. An Alternative American Story

"What do you think of my idea"? Ruth asked.

"I think your better off in a creative writing class," Sula said with a chuckle. "Don't you dare write any of that on your history exam. You'll get laughed out of class. You know George Washington died in 1776 trying to cross the Delaware. He wasn't our first president, everybody knows Abraham Lincoln he was. Anyway, what's with that silly song you keep singing, '⁵stars and stripes forever?' You know our flag has only two giant stars."

"Sula, Lincoln wouldn't have been president at all if General Grant would not have disappeared three weeks before the 1866 election, but that's not the point. What if George Washington *had* crossed the Delaware? What if *we* had won the Colonial War? I wonder how different things would have been? We might have been our own country in 1776, ninety-eight years before the Continental War of Independence. What if we had no East and West? What if we were living in a state right now, instead of in a territory?"

"Ruth," Sula said in exasperation, "Go no farther. Get through to you is impossible! I'm going elsewhere too study.

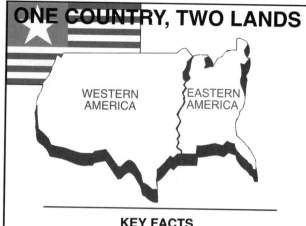

ONE COUNTRY, TWO LANDS

WESTERN AMERICA

EASTERN AMERICA

KEY FACTS

- 1 country with 2 territories since the 1866 victory over Great Britain in Continental War of Independence
- representative government, with Congress and president
- combined economy ranks 3rd in world in productivity, debt
- population of 260 million ranks 6th in world

The map and facts shown above describe the country that Ruth and Sula call home.

I'll see you later. Good luck on your test. You'll need it." Sula left her patience at an end.

In her favorite notebook, Ruth sat down and began to write her story. Patriot's Tale began as follows: "It all started on a cold night in December. The Delaware River was cold but not frozen and visibility was good. Hoping for the best, General Washington ordered the surprise attack to commence..."

Find the 18 errors in this activity.
There are no errors in the illustration or the caption.

29. An A+ for C++

I've been giving my future career a lot of thought and now decided that I could best put my technical skills to use by becoming an educator. As a teacher, my students should be able to expect lessons with immediate feedback for her answers. The problem is is that the increasing size of classes are making such goals more difficulter than ever. That's why I plan to program the lessons myself in the C++ language (as learned from professor Duong). With a computer program, students could do lessons at their own pace; the computer would not only ask questions tireless but also tell whether they are correct.

I'm now creating a program (a part of which you can see in the illustration at right for identifying state capitals. The program will contain the following; a "loop," which keeps asking for the correct input until it is entered; "if/else" statements (one of which is shown in the diagram;) and some "while" statements. When students pick choice two, Denver, as the capital of California, they won't have to wait for me to tell them, "You're full of beans!" That's what my program will display.

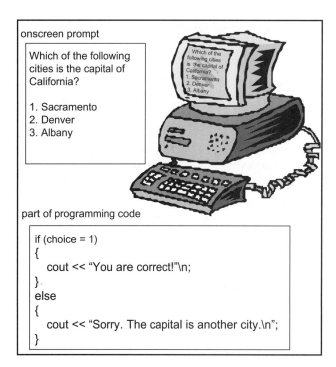

onscreen prompt

Which of the following cities is the capital of California?

1. Sacramento
2. Denver
3. Albany

part of programming code

```
if (choice = 1)
{
    cout << "You are correct!"\n;
}
else
{
    cout << "Sorry. The capital is another city.\n";
}
```

Here is part of my program. At the top is a question the student would see on the screen. Below the question are "if/else" statements from the program that allow for feedback depending on the input (choice 1, 2, or 3). If the user picks 1, the screen will show the words after the first "cout <<" expression in the code above. For any other answer, the user will see the words after the second "cout <<" expression. I'll also use at least one "loop" and some "while" statements.

Programming is such fun that I am anxious to take my study of C++ even farther. I'm sure that it will greatly benefit both my students and I!

**Find the 16 errors in this activity.
There are no errors in the illustration or the caption.**

---

30. Biking Trail Debate

Last night, the city council heard arguments for and against the proposed mountain bike trail and training program. (Trail design would mimic the Bikersville, Ark trail built in 1994). As expected, Dan Jones of DJ Trail Bikes came out in favor. "Mountain bike riders are numerous," he contended, and they deserve a safe place to ride.

Gabe Cordova thought the trail would be "useless for most of we taxpayers." Also opposing the issue, Lucy McGovern voiced concerns of some safety-minded citizens. "We are against the trail because mountain biking promotes careless behavior," she said. "Don't you remember what happened in May of 98 at that impromptu, mens' contest"?

Teen biker Gwen Schaffer then expressed her view. "That was caused by some local guy yelling, You're a liar and a cheat!" to another spectator and then pushing him in front of a racer," she argued.

"She's right," said captain Armelando of the police force, "and accept for that fiasco, the only problems have been caused by lack of facilities. Besides we can prevent careless biking by requiring that each user passes the safety course."

Several other citizens followed in expressing their views on the proposal. In

In May 1998, Won Kim had crested the hill and was about to stabilize when a spectator, pushed by a rowdy out-of-towner, fell onto the trail. Kim swerved to avoid a collision and went down in a heap, separating his shoulder.

spite of cost and safety concerns, however, most attendees were proponents. In summary, the following pluses were cited

1) safety through training
2) convenience of location
3) outlet for teenagers' energy

Views will continue to be heard during the next two week's meetings. The council will vote on the issue in three weeks.

Find the 18 errors in this activity.
There are no errors in the illustration or the caption.

31. A View to a Job

January 12, 2006

Angelique Giroux Managing Editor
Snapshot
Washington Square
White Plains NY, 10609

Dear Ms. Giroux,

As a magazine editor, you want a photographer you can count on to provide top-quality photos and also meet deadlines. I can do both. My name is Kamilah Desai, and I am applying for the special assignment advertised in *Snapshot*.

As you can see from my enclosed resume I have traveled the world in search of interesting photo opportunities. My most recent assignment was a freelance job for an advertising agency in Hong Kong. I shot scenes of the fish markets to illustrated a series of magazine ads, that stressed the importance of tradition in a technologically advanced world. Doing a job as it has been done for hundreds of years, the photos showed people etched in almost surreal timelessness. I won an Eastman award for this. The whole advertising team were proud.

My favorite assignment so far has been the four years I spent as the Senior Photographer for *Utah Illustrated*, published by the state travel association. The opportunities to capture nature on film is still very abundant in Utah. I found

On January 12, 2006, Kamilah Desai applied for a job with *Snapshot* magazine. She sent the above photos and business card, as well as her resume.

that a creative approach to such well photographed targets as Bryce Canyon and Trolley Square can yield photos of places that, at the same time, not only seem familiar but also new.

Please find enclosed these three things a packet of sample photographs I have taken, my resume, and my business card. If you wish to contact me immediately, please send me an e-mail message at kdesai@adn.com.

Thank you for your time and consideration. I hope to here from you soon.

Sincerely

Kamilah Desai

Kamilah Desai

Find the 17 errors in this activity.
There are no errors in the illustration or the caption.

32. Succeeding in Business

Many people think they could create a successful business, but few make the dream a reality. The formula for growing a business may seem simple (you plan you work you succeed), but don't be fooled. If success was easy, most of us would be wealthy! Long and grueling are the road to success, and you must often work like a dog—a dog who is racing against the fastest of competitors!

Do you have what it takes to be a successful entrepreneur? Wanda soul proprietor of Wanda's Widgets, has found the following traits essential for her success in business.

Positive Attitude: Can you remain optimistic through hard times? It helps to be a confident cheerful owner. A delay in profits have frustrated many competitors, however, Wanda has stuck it out. It is her who now enjoys a flourishing trade.

Resources: Have you saved enough seed" money to support the business for a few years? Many businesses take several years to become profitable. Wanda's Widgets, for example, was not profitable until the third year. She had to be thrifty.

People Skills: Do you get along and communicate well with people? Many companies failures can be traced to miscommunication and strife. Wanda was always clear and fair in dealing with an employee, knowing that they were one of the company's greatest assets.

Though it took hard work, Wanda made her dream come true. In the chart, the dashed line shows expected profit and the black line shows actual profit realized by her company for the years given.

Knowledge: Do you have enough knowledge about your product and how to market it? Wanda already had experience and knowledge, what she didn't know she learned in night classes.

Need to Achieve: Do you want success so badly that you would do anything necessary to get it? Only the strongest desire will keep you from quitting. Wanda thought of giving up; however, when her company announces their annual profit, she's glad she has stuck with it!

Having review the above requirements, you should have an idea of your own potential for business. Will yours be the next multimillion-dollar success?

Find the 18 errors in this activity.
There are no errors in the illustration or the caption.

---

33. A Patent Lie?

Thaddeus related the following story at the June, 99 Hoax Masters Club meeting:

"Driving home last week, my eyes met with an unusual sight: a huge saucer was spinning north, and on the ground was a one-eyed alien, thumbing a ride. She planned either to stay on Earth awhile or had other means of returning home. I stopped.

"The alien was soon settled into my car her case balanced carefully on her lap. She said her name was 'Aaarveugh', which, in English, is Doris. She was very similar to we humans with some exceptions. She had the extra eye, and she had much better visual dexterity than us. She could see in any direction, individually or in a group, by swivelling the eye stems.

"How would you like to have my visual abilities? she queried. I was interested.

"'We have identified the gene site for the trait, and it is on the X chromosome. If you drink a bottle of the chromosomes and special enzymes, you can be sure that the gene will attach itself to your DNA.' It sounded great, but I wondered if there was a catch? There was.

"'We have heard of the numerous lawyers, as well as the great interest in self-improvement, here on Earth. In return for a vial, you must do several things: find a patent attorney for me; ingest the chromosomes, along with the

This is what Thaddeus saw as he headed north on the highway; the ship was coming directly toward him. He picked up the alien and learned that others like her were being dropped off at other planets to show their product.

enzymes, and demonstrate the results to fellow humans. We will market this product extensively.'

"The alien and me made a pact; she rummaged between the bottles and selected one for me.

"I have agreed to spread the word about these special bottles to you, my fellow Hoax Masters. I'm sure you'll all want one now that you've heard my story of the 'X vials.'

Thaddeus concluded his presentation by sweeping his eyes 360 degrees around the room.

Find the 18 errors in this activity.
There are no errors in the illustration or the caption.

ANSWERS

This answer key provides the following information for each activity: the number and types of errors, a paragraph using superscribed numbers to show the locations of the errors, a corresponding number key explaining the errors, and the corrected paragraph.

Note that in the error count below, a run-on sentence or a sentence fragment is counted as one error even though the correction may require two changes, e.g., adding or deleting a period and a capital letter.

The errors in English mechanics in *Editor in Chief® C2* have been geared to correspond to an advanced-level English curriculum. For further information about the rules of grammar, usage, and punctuation covered in this book, see the *Guide* pp. 81–130.

1. Using Figurative Language

13 errors—1 content; 2 grammar; 7 punctuation; 1 usage

Using Figurative Language Errors

If you have ever wrote[1] a description, you may have used figures of speech known as similes and metaphors. These gems can improve anyones'[2] writing.

A simile or metaphor allow[3] the reader to visualize more clearly who or what the author is describing. Using simile, the writer compares two unlike items directly, using the words *like* or *as*;[4] "He runs like the wind" or "The runner is as swift as the wind." The comparison in a metaphor is implied—,[5] and the writer states that one thing *is* another (though it is clearly not:)[6] "His heart is a stone." Either type of figurative language create[7] a vivid image in the reader's mind.

Examples of simile and metaphor is[8] found throughout literature. In his play *Romeo and Juliet*, Shakespeare wrote a metaphor comparing the young couples'[9] new love to a budding flower:

> This bud of love...,
> May prove a beauteous flower
>   when next we meet.

Herman Melville used this metaphor[10] to describe the whale in his book *Moby Dick*:

> The glittering mouth yawned beneath the boat like an open-doored marble tomb.

It can be easy to overdo figurative language. Our daily speech is fill[11] with expressions used so often,[12] that they have become cliches. Avoid writing such over-used expressions as "neat as a pin" and "slept like a baby." It's also better not to mix figures of speech; the resulting images are often illogical: "I'm keeping my eye on America's pulse, and I can feel the beat!"

The next time you write a story or a description, try using figurative language. It's "a piece of cake!"[13]

1. have ever *written*—Grammar: past participle (used with present perfect tense [have written]) **[3.29, 3.36]**
2. *anyone's*—Punctuation: 's used with possessive indefinite pronoun **[5.7]**
3. metaphor *allows*—Usage: agreement of verb with closer of two subjects joined by *or* **[4.6]**
4. *as:*—Punctuation: colon introduces words that explain or illustrate **[5.12]**
5. *implied,*—Punctuation: avoid multiple punctuation **[5.73]**
   (Acceptable: *implied—*)
6. *not):*—Punctuation: colon outside parenthesis **[5.14]**
7. *creates*—Usage: agreement of verb with indefinite pronoun (either/creates) **[4.8]**
8. *are*—Usage: agreement of verb with subject (separated) (examples are) **[4.3]**

9. *couple's* —Punctuation: *'s* used with singular possessive **[5.4]**

10. *simile*—Content: see caption **[2.1]**

11. is *filled* with—Grammar: past participle (in present tense passive voice) **[3.29, 3.36]**
    (Acceptable: is *full of* expressions)

12. *often that*—Punctuation: comma unnecessary (splits dependent clause) **[5.41 k]**

13. *cake"!* —Punctuation: exclamation point outside quotes when exclamation is part of whole sentence **[5.45]**

Using Figurative Language Corrected

If you have ever written a description, you may have used figures of speech known as similes and metaphors. These gems can improve anyone's writing.

A simile or metaphor allows the reader to visualize more clearly who or what the author is describing. Using simile, the writer compares two unlike items directly, using the words *like* or *as*: "He runs like the wind" or "The runner is as swift as the wind." The comparison in a metaphor is implied, and the writer states that one thing *is* another (though it is clearly not): "His heart is a stone." Either type of figurative language creates a vivid image in the reader's mind.

Examples of simile and metaphor are found throughout literature. In his play *Romeo and Juliet*, Shakespeare wrote a metaphor comparing the young couple's new love to a budding flower:

> This bud of love...,
> May prove a beauteous flower
> when next we meet.

Herman Melville used this simile to describe the whale in his book *Moby Dick*:

> The glittering mouth yawned beneath the boat like an open-doored marble tomb.

It can be easy to overdo figurative language. Our daily speech is filled with expressions used so often that they have become cliches. Avoid writing such over-used expressions as "neat as a pin" and "slept like a baby." It's also better not to mix figures of speech; the resulting images are often illogical: "I'm keeping my eye on America's pulse, and I can feel the beat!"

The next time you write a story or a description, try using figurative language. It's "a piece of cake"!

2. Skeleton Crew

14 errors—2 content; 4 grammar; 5 punctuation; 2 spelling; 2 usage

Skeleton Crew Errors

On the night the museum paintings came alive, the skeletons from several paintings used the leg bones and hip[1] bones to play baseball. Using the leg bones for bats and the kneecap bones for baseballs, they plaid[2] for several hours in the main lobby, taking turns at bat.

In the room east of the lobby, other skeletons danced to the sounds of Boney Goodman and the Femurs. Some skeletons had to bone up on his[3] steps but were back dancing soon.

In the room to the west of the lobby, still other skeletons practiced their card-playing skills with cards they had borrow[4] from a painting full of dogs. One skeleton whom[5] was a little rusty was told to found[6] a different game. [7]After one especially bonehead hand.

It was the baseball game, however, that was the most popular. Each side had the full team of five[8] players, and the teams took turns pitching. Ground balls took sharp hops,[9] when the bone bounced high off the wooden floor. Outfielders had trouble catching some line drives because they didn't have gloves. You [10]had to really[10] hand it to them for trying, though. Caution [11]to be sure[11] was a factor on some plays. For instance, no one dared slide into a base for fear of going to pieces. Still, the skeletons enjoyed themselves immensely, playing into the we[12] hours of the morning.

Finally, being game-weary and bone-tired[13] they set about their cleanup so that when the museum workers'[14] returned, they would see nothing amiss.

1. *kneecap bones*—Content: see caption and illustration **[2.1]**
2. *played*—Spelling **[6.7]**
3. *their*—Usage: agreement of possessive pronoun with noun in number (skeletons/their) **[4.1]**
4. had *borrowed*—Grammar: past participle (used in past perfect tense) **[3.29, 3.36]**
5. *who*—Grammar: pronoun *who* as subject of adjective clause **[3.26]**
6. *find*—Grammar: infinitive **[3.39]**
7. *game after*—Punctuation: sentence fragment **[5.82]**
8. *nine*—Content: see caption **[2.1]**
9. *hops when*—Punctuation: comma unnecessary when dependent clause follows main clause **[5.41 l]**
10. *really had to* hand—Grammar: don't split infinitive **[3.40]**
11. *Caution, to be sure,*—Punctuation: comma used with sentence interrupter **[5.28]**
12. *wee*—Spelling **[6.1]**
13. *Finally, being game-weary and bone-tired,*—Punctuation: comma used with nonessential participial phrase **[5.31]**
14. *workers*—Punctuation: unnecessary apostrophe **[5.3]**

Skeleton Crew Corrected

On the night the museum paintings came alive, the skeletons from several paintings used the leg bones and kneecap bones to play baseball. Using the leg bones for bats and the kneecap bones for baseballs, they played for several hours in the main lobby, taking turns at bat.

In the room east of the lobby, other skeletons danced to the sounds of Boney Goodman and the Femurs. Some skeletons had to bone up on their steps but were back dancing soon.

In the room to the west of the lobby, still other skeletons practiced their card-playing skills with cards they had borrowed from a painting full of dogs. One skeleton who was a little rusty was told to find a different game after one especially bonehead hand.

It was the baseball game, however, that was the most popular. Each side had the full team of nine players, and the teams took turns pitching. Ground balls took sharp hops when the bone bounced high off the wooden floor. Outfielders had trouble catching some line drives because they didn't have gloves. You really had to hand it to them for trying, though. Caution, to be sure, was a factor on some plays. For instance, no one dared slide into a base for fear of going to pieces. Still, the skeletons enjoyed themselves immensely, playing into the wee hours of the morning.

Finally, being game-weary and bone-tired, they set about their cleanup so that when the museum workers returned, they would see nothing amiss.

3. The Leopard Speaks

14 errors—1 content; 2 capitalization; 5 grammar; 2 spelling; 4 usage

The Leopard Speaks Errors

It's a[1] honor to be chosen;
Yes, your Leopard King[2] I'll be.
As judge I'll be most principaled[3]—
Uninterested[4] as can be.

My background may be[5], like,[5] spotty,
But, in fact, I have a nose
For sniffing out the fairest way
With which to [6]have interposed[6].

From the very least noteworthy
To the more[7] magnificent,
All cats will be respected—
No matter what they're[8] scents.

Who is more equipped than me[9]
The cat laws to create?
I'll carry them to other Cats[10]
To who[11] we all relate.

Enough you've had of business now;
Let's talk of racing games.
The members running furthest[12]
Join the Leopards' Hall of Fame.

We shall lie[13] out a giant feast,
When races have been run.
I will proclaim a holiday
Called [14]day of leopard fun[14]!

1. *an* honor—Grammar: article *an* before vowel sound **[3.5]**
2. *Queen*—Content: see caption **[2.1]**
3. *principled*—Spelling **[6.1]**
4. *Disinterested*—Usage: word pair (disinterested/uninterested) **[4.18]**
5. be ~~like~~ spotty—Usage: unnecessary word **[4.19]**
6. to *interpose*—Grammar: infinitive **[3.39]**
7. *most* magnificent—Grammar: superlative adjective **[3.6]**
8. *their*—Spelling **[6.1]**
9. *I*—Grammar: pronoun following *than* in incomplete construction **[3.24]**
10. *cats*—Capital: unnecessary (not used as proper noun) **[1.4]**
11. *whom*—Grammar: pronoun *whom* used as object **[3.26]**
12. *farthest*—Usage: word pair (furthest/farthest) **[4.18]**
13. *lay*—Usage: word pair (lay/lie) **[4.18]**
14. *Day of Leopard Fun*—Capital: holiday **[1.11]**

The Leopard Speaks Corrected

It's an honor to be chosen;
Yes, your Leopard Queen I'll be.
As judge I'll be most principled—
Disinterested as can be.

My background may be spotty,
But, in fact, I have a nose

For sniffing out the fairest way
With which to interpose.

From the very least noteworthy
To the most magnificent,
All cats will be respected—
No matter what their scents.

Who is more equipped than I
The cat laws to create?
I'll carry them to other cats
To whom we all relate.

Enough you've had of business now;
Let's talk of racing games.
The members running farthest
Join the Leopards' Hall of Fame.

We shall lay out a giant feast,
When races have been run.
I will proclaim a holiday
Called Day of Leopard Fun!

4. Keeping a Legend Alive

13 errors—1 content; 1 grammar; 8 punctuation; 1 spelling; 2 usage

Keeping a Legend Alive Errors

One of the favorite races of distance runners is the marathon. For some runners, the marathon is the ultimate test of endurence[1],[2] for others, it's a stepping stone to even longer races. Some is[3] 50 or even 100 miles long, but the principal yardstick by which all races are measured continues to be:[4] the marathon.

The modern marathon began in the 1896 Olympics, held in Athens, and has been a part of the Olympics ever since[5] The event commemorates the legendary 25-mile run of Pheidippides northeast[6] from Marathon to Athens to let the Athenians at home know of their warriors[7] great victory over the Persians in 490 B.C. The Athenians, despite having 4,000 less[8] soldiers than the invaders, halted the first large-scale Persian invasion of Greece.

Though the [9]runner, Pheidippides,[9] ran 25 miles, today's marathoners run 26.2 miles. The longer distance was first run at the 1908 Olympics in England (when the organizers wanted the race to start at Windsor Castle and finish in front of the royal box at the stadium in London[10] and [11]was standardize[11] at the 1924 Olympics in France.

Well-known United States marathon sites include New York, N.Y.,[12] Boston, Mass;[13] and Big Sur, Calif.

1. *endurance*—Spelling **[6.7]**
2. *endurance;*—Punctuation: semicolon separates main clauses joined without coordinating conjunction **[5.68]**
3. *are*—Usage: agreement of verb with indefinite pronoun **[4.8]**
4. *be*—Punctuation: colon unnecessary **[5.13]**
5. *since.*—Punctuation: period used after declarative sentence **[5.52]**
6. *southwest*—Content: see illustration **[2.1]**
7. *warriors'*—Punctuation: apostrophe used with possessive of plural ending in *s* **[5.5]**
8. *fewer*—Usage: word pair (less/fewer) **[4.18]**
9. *runner Pheidippides*—Punctuation: commas unnecessary with essential appositive **[5.41 i]**
10. *London)*—Punctuation: parentheses used (in pairs) to enclose supplementary words **[5.49]**
11. was *standardized*—Grammar: past participle (used in past tense passive voice) **[3.29, 3.36]**
12. *N.Y.;*—Punctuation: semicolon separates items (in a series) containing commas **[5.70]**
13. *Mass.*—Punctuation: period after abbreviation **[5.53]**

Keeping a Legend Alive Corrected

One of the favorite races of distance runners is the marathon. For some runners, the marathon is the ultimate test of endurance; for others, it's a stepping stone to even longer races. Some are 50 or even 100 miles long, but the principal yardstick by which all races are measured continues to be the marathon.

The modern marathon began in the 1896 Olympics, held in Athens, and has been a part of the Olympics ever since. The event commemorates the legendary 25-mile run of Pheidippides southwest from Marathon to Athens to let the Athenians at home know of their warriors' great victory over the Persians in 490 B.C. The Athenians, despite having 4,000 fewer soldiers than the invaders, halted the first large-scale Persian invasion of Greece.

Though the runner Pheidippides ran 25 miles, today's marathoners run 26.2 miles. The longer distance was first run at the 1908 Olympics in England (when the organizers wanted the race to start at Windsor Castle and finish in front of the royal box at the stadium in London) and was standardized at the 1924 Olympics in France.

Well-known United States marathon sites include New York, N.Y.; Boston, Mass.; and Big Sur, Calif.

5. Cross-Country Adventure

14 errors—1 content; 1 capitalization; 1 grammar; 7 punctuation; 4 usage

Cross-Country Adventure Errors

Andre heads into an unmarked area, drawn by the huge drifts of untouched powder. The previous nights'[1] storm has left almost a foot of fresh snow. As he slides along the base of the hill, he yells for the sheer joy of it, not knowing disaster is eminent[2]. His echoing voice sets off a responding roar in the slope above him, and mountains of snow come tumbling down the hillside[3] catching him like a huge wave. He rolls and tumbles down the slope, sinking deeper and deeper. [4]Inside the snowy wave. His skis go flying, torn from his feet by the force of the avalanche.

When he stops moving, everything is still[5] nothing is around him but the endless white; he is buried beneath the snow, his limbs askew from the impact. Can he move anything at all? Luckily, one arm lies close beside his head. He wriggles his fingers until he is able to clear a tiny air hole. He must be close to the surface, but the more he struggles, the more firmer[6] he becomes wedged.

He now regrets having left the unmarked[7] trail. He knows that he didn't tell anyone where he was going,[8] and that there is little chance of another skier coming this way. How will anyone find him? He doesn't know how long he can remain buried this way; the wet snow is already beginning to soak through his clothes, and he is so cold,[9] that his entire body throbs. "It's better than being numb, though," he thinks.

Either the cold or the lack of oxygen or both causes[10] him to drift in and out of consciousness. Suddenly, hands reach down into the snow, grab him, and pull him up. He gasps for air as he reaches the surface.

The rescue team is[11] relieved that they have found him in time. A snowmobiler who ventured into the same area had found Andre's skis sticking out of the snow and alerted the ski patrol,[12] "I'm glad to be alive," Andre tells his Dad[13]. "I will never take Mother Nature for granted again[14] Pop."

1. *night's* storm—Punctuation: *'s* used with singular possessive **[5.4]**
2. *imminent*—Usage: word pair (imminent/eminent) **[4.18]**
3. *hillside,* catching—Punctuation: comma used with nonessential participial phrase **[5.31]**
4. *deeper inside*—Punctuation: sentence fragment **[5.82]**
5. *still. Nothing*—Punctuation: run-on sentence **[5.81]**

(Acceptable: *still; nothing...white. He*)
6. more *firmly*—Grammar: comparative adverb **[3.6]**
7. *marked*—Content: see caption **[2.1]** (Acceptable: *designated*)
8. *going* and that—Punctuation: comma unnecessary between dependent clauses **[5.41 o]**
9. *cold that*—Punctuation: comma unnecessary with essential clause **[5.41 i]**
10. both *cause*—Usage: agreement of verb with closer of two or more subjects joined by *or* **[4.6]**
11. *team are*—Usage: agreement of verb with collective subject used in a plural sense **[4.4]**
12. *patrol.*—Punctuation: period used after declarative sentence **[5.52]**
13. his *dad.*—Capital: unnecessary (not used as proper name) **[1.4]**
14. *again,* Pop—Punctuation: comma used with noun of address **[5.27]**

Cross-Country Adventure Corrected

Andre heads into an unmarked area, drawn by the huge drifts of untouched powder. The previous night's storm has left almost a foot of fresh snow. As he slides along the base of the hill, he yells for the sheer joy of it, not knowing disaster is imminent. His echoing voice sets off a responding roar in the slope above him, and mountains of snow come tumbling down the hillside, catching him like a huge wave. He rolls and tumbles down the slope, sinking deeper and deeper inside the snowy wave. His skis go flying, torn from his feet by the force of the avalanche.

When he stops moving, everything is still. Nothing is around him but the endless white; he is buried beneath the snow, his limbs askew from the impact. Can he move anything at all? Luckily, one arm lies close beside his head. He wriggles his fingers until he is able to clear a tiny air hole. He must be close to the surface, but the more he struggles, the more firmly he becomes wedged.

He now regrets having left the marked trail. He knows that he didn't tell anyone where he was going and that there is little chance of another skier coming this way. How will anyone find him? He doesn't know how long he can remain buried this way; the wet snow is already beginning to soak through his clothes, and he is so cold that his entire body throbs. "It's better than being numb, though," he thinks.

Either the cold or the lack of oxygen or both cause him to drift in and out of consciousness. Suddenly, hands reach down into the snow, grab him, and pull him up. He gasps for air as he reaches the surface.

The rescue team are relieved that they have found him in time. A snowmobiler who ventured into the same area had found Andre's skis sticking out of the snow and alerted the ski patrol. "I'm glad to be alive," Andre tells his dad. "I will never take Mother Nature for granted again, Pop."

6. A Capital Challenge

14 errors—2 content; 3 capitalization; 2 grammar; 4 punctuation; 1 spelling; 2 usage

A Capital Challenge Errors

"To find the first of six[1] destinations, start at the building that honors are[2] first president[3]" the instructions read. Leroy went to the Washington Monument. "Climb the steps, and stop at the seventy-sixth step. Pickup[4] the piece of paper taped to the handrail, and climb back down. Hold the piece of paper up to a mirror to see where to go next[5]"

Holding the paper up to a mirror, Leroy saw the words "War" and "Wall," so he went to the Vietnam Veterans Memorial. It took a few minutes to walked[6] the long way along the wall, and he saw [7]on their faces many people studying the names on the wall with faraway looks[7]. Under the [8]rock, at the end of the long list of names,[8] was his last set of instructions:

"[9]find the second mirror, go to what you see reflected, and read the words of a famous speech. Return to where you started, and say the first six words of the speech. You're done."

This last clue was a real[10] tough one, but Leroy finally figured out that the second mirror was the Reflecting Pool and that what he saw in it was the reflection of the Lincoln Memorial. He went to the [11]Memorial and read the [12]gettysburg address[12,13]which is carved into rock many feet high. He took the most direct route, [14]over the Potomac River,[14] to his first destination and recited the first six words of Lincoln's speech: "Four score and seven years ago." Leroy had finished the scavenger hunt.

1. *four* — Content: see map and/or caption **[2.1]**
2. *our* — Usage: word pair (are/our) **[4.18]**
3. *president,"* — Punctuation: comma separates quote from speaker **[5.39]**
4. *pick up* — Spelling **[6.6]**
5. *next."* — Punctuation: period inside quotation marks **[5.54]**
6. to *walk* — Grammar: infinitive **[3.39]** (Acceptable: *walking*)
7. *many people with faraway looks on their faces studying the names on the wall* — Usage: misplaced modifier **[4.15]**
8. *rock* at the end of the long list of *names* was — Punctuation: commas unnecessary with essential phrase **[5.41 i]**
9. *"Find* — Capital: first word in quotation **[1.2]**
10. *really* — Grammar: adverb modifies adjective **[3.4]**
11. *memorial* — Capital: unnecessary (not used as proper noun) **[1.4]**
12. *Gettysburg Address* — Capital: proper noun **[1.4]**
13. *Address, which* — Punctuation: comma used with nonessential adjective phrase **[5.31]**

14. *past the Reflecting Pool,—*Content: see map **[2.1]**

A Capital Challenge Corrected

"To find the first of four destinations, start at the building that honors our first president," the instructions read. Leroy went to the Washington Monument. "Climb the steps, and stop at the seventy-sixth step. Pick up the piece of paper taped to the handrail, and climb back down. Hold the piece of paper up to a mirror to see where to go next."

Holding the paper up to a mirror, Leroy saw the words "War" and "Wall," so he went to the Vietnam Veterans Memorial. It took a few minutes to walk the long way along the wall, and he saw many people with faraway looks on their faces studying the names on the wall. Under a rock at the end of the long list of names was his last set of instructions: "Find the second mirror, go to what you see reflected, and read the words of a famous speech. Return to where you started, and say the first six words of the speech. You're done."

This last clue was a really tough one, but Leroy finally figured out that the second mirror was the Reflecting Pool and that what he saw in it was the reflection of the Lincoln Memorial. He went to the memorial and read the Gettysburg Address, which is carved into rock many feet high. He took the most direct route, past the Reflecting Pool, to his first destination and recited the first six words of Lincoln's speech: "Four score and seven years ago." Leroy had finished the scavenger hunt.

7. Running for Fun and Fitness

14 errors—1 content; 1 capitalization; 7 punctuation; 1 spelling; 4 usage

Running for Fun and Fitness Errors

Running is a good way to improve your overall fitness,[1] the affects[2] of such exer-cise can be dramatic, offering benefits to your muscles, your blood flow, and [3]how you think[3].

To start with, running increases the anaerobic[4] capacity of your lungs. That is, you can breathe in more air each time you inhale. This[5] makes your heart stronger and also increases the flow of oxygen though[6] your bloodstream, helping flush harmful[7] unwanted bacteria,[8] and chemicals out of your system.

Running also helps you burn fat. The thing to remember, though, is that the faster you run, the more carbohydrates you burn. To take off the fat, you need to run more slowly and for a longer period of time. Your body should be able to sustain a longer run if its[9] a slower run. The question is[10] how[11] slowly should you run? The key is to keep moving. Even if you think you're going too slowly, you're still getting the cardiovascular benefits that running provides.

Running can help you escape the demands of everyday living, enabling you to think of things,[12] other than a job or school. Running can also clear your head and offer you a new way to look at a situation. As a result, both body and mind gets[13] a workout.

Running can be good for your health and is also an enjoyable way to spend time. As someone once said[14] "Time flies when you're having fun running."

1. *fitness. The—*Punctuation: period corrects comma splice **[5.81]**
2. *effects—*Usage: word pair (affect/effect) **[4.18]**
3. *your thinking—*Usage: parallel structure **[4.12]**
   (Acceptable: *your mind, your brain, etc.*)
4. *aerobic—*Content: see caption **[2.1]**
5. *This increased aerobic capacity—*Usage: ambiguous pronoun reference **[3.19]**
6. *through—*Spelling **[6.1]**
7. *harmful,—*Punctuation: comma separates coordinate adjectives **[5.24]**

8. *bacteria*—Punctuation: comma unnecessary (splits adverb phrase) **[5.41 j, m]**

9. *it's*—Punctuation: apostrophe used with contraction **[5.1]**

10. *is,*—Punctuation: comma introduces direct question within sentence **[5.35]**

11. *How*—Capital: first word of question within a sentence **[1.3]**

12. *things* other—Punctuation: comma unnecessary (splits adverb phrase) **[5.41 j]**

13. *get*—Usage: agreement of verb with compound subjects joined by and (body and mind/get) **[4.6]**

14. *said,*—Punctuation: comma separates quote from speaker **[5.39]**

Running for Fun and Fitness Corrected

Running is a good way to improve your overall fitness. The effects of such exercise can be dramatic, offering benefits to your muscles, your blood flow, and your mind.

To start with, running increases the aerobic capacity of your lungs. That is, you can breathe in more air each time you inhale. This increased aerobic capacity makes your heart stronger and also increases the flow of oxygen through your bloodstream, helping flush harmful, unwanted bacteria and chemicals out of your system.

Running also helps you burn fat. The thing to remember, though, is that the faster you run, the more carbohydrates you burn. To take off the fat, you need to run more slowly and for a longer period of time. Your body should be able to sustain a longer run if it's a slower run. The question is, How slow should you run? The key is to keep moving. Even if you think you're going too slowly, you're still getting the cardiovascular benefits that running provides.

Running can help you escape the demands of everyday living, enabling you to think of things other than a job or school. Running can also clear your head and offer you a new way to look at a situation.

As a result, both body and mind get a workout.

Running can be good for your health and is also an enjoyable way to spend time. As someone once said, "Time flies when you're having fun running."

8. Scheduling Conflict

15 errors—2 content; 1 capitalization; 6 grammar; 4 punctuation; 1 spelling; 1 usage

Scheduling Conflict Errors

Diane had a big-time problem on her hands: one of her stars was leaving.

Diane was head of programming for FAVE-TV, and she needed a Fall[1] replacement for Michael Baker, whom[2] was leaving the highly rated "True Crime" series for a career in movies. Everybody else in the management circle was holding their[3] breath, but it looked like Baker was on his way out.

One option, of course, was to continue the show with a new host. However, Baker had become immensely popular in certain big-city markets. It was him[4] who had convinced many people to watch the low-rated "On the Police Beat," at 9 o[5] clock, just so they could be right on time for "True Crime" at 10 and would'nt[6] have to leave [7]"Movie of the Week"[7] or "Thad's Science Fiction Theater" halfway through. Advertisers had pick[8] up on this trend and started paying for time during "On the Police Beat," so the show stayed on the air. Baker was the real draw, and it was an open secret to whomever[9] was in the know.

None of the network's four half-hour shows, which aired from [10]8 to 10 P.M.[10], were top-rated shows, although,[11] they were all near the top. What could compete with "I Love Lucido?"[12] It was "True Crime" that was the real moneymaker for the relatively new FAVE-TV, which begun[13] as a regional network just 10 years ago.

The top brass had offered Baker alot[14] more money, reportedly double his salary, but he hadn't budged. He already had creative control of the show, which had whetted his appetite for directing big-budget motion pictures. He also knew he will[15] be able to command a higher salary in the movie industry.

The programming directors at the other three major networks were smiling, but for Diane the question remained: "Where was the next Michael Baker?"

1. *fall*—Capital: unnecessary in season (unless personified) **[1.12]**
2. *who*—Grammar: pronoun *who* as subject of adjective clause **[3.26]**
3. *his or her*—Usage: agreement of possessive pronoun with indefinite pronoun **[4.9]**
4. *he*—Grammar: nominative case used with the verb "to be" **[3.23]**
5. *o' clock*—Punctuation: apostrophe used with contraction **[5.1]**
6. *wouldn't*—Punctuation: apostrophe used with contraction (replaces missing letters) **[5.1]**
7. *"Mystery Movie"*—Content: see illustration **[2.1]**
8. had *picked*—Grammar: past participle (used in past perfect tense) **[3.29, 3.36]**
9. *whoever*—Grammar: pronoun *whoever* as subject of noun phrase **[3.26]**
10. *7 to 9 P.M.*—Content: see illustration **[2.1]**
11. *although they*—Punctuation: unnecessary comma (splits an adverb phrase) **[5.41 j]**
12. *Lucido"?*—Punctuation: question mark outside quotation marks when it doesn't apply to quoted material **[5.59]**
13. *had* begun—Grammar: helping verb (used in past perfect tense) **[3.29, 3.33]**
14. *a lot*—Spelling **[6.6]**
15. *would*—Grammar: after past tense verb, use *would,* not *will* **[3.31]**

Scheduling Conflict Corrected

Diane had a big-time problem on her hands: one of her stars was leaving.

Diane was head of programming for FAVE-TV, and she needed a fall replacement for Michael Baker, who was leaving the highly rated "True Crime" series for a career in movies. Everybody else in the management circle was holding his or her breath, but it looked like Baker was on his way out.

One option, of course, was to continue the show with a new host. However, Baker had become immensely popular in certain big-city markets. It was he who had convinced many people to watch the low-rated "On the Police Beat," at 9 o' clock, just so they could be right on time for "True Crime" at 10 and wouldn't have to leave "Mystery Movie" or "Thad's Science Fiction Theater" halfway through. Advertisers had picked up on this trend and started paying for time during "On the Police Beat," so the show stayed on the air. Baker was the real draw, and it was an open secret to whoever was in the know.

None of the network's four half-hour shows, which aired from 7 to 9 P.M., were top-rated shows, although they were all near the top. What could compete with "I Love Lucido"? It was "True Crime" that was the real moneymaker for the relatively new FAVE-TV, which had begun as a regional network just 10 years ago.

The top brass had offered Baker a lot more money, reportedly double his salary, but he hadn't budged. He already had creative control of the show, which had whetted his appetite for directing big-budget motion pictures. He also knew he would be able to command a higher salary in the movie industry.

The programming directors at the other three major networks were smiling, but for Diane the question remained: "Where was the next Michael Baker?"

9. Enlightened about Electrons

15 errors—1 content; 3 grammar; 7 punctuation; 2 spelling; 2 usage

Enlightened about Electrons Errors

"Whats[1] the big deal about those particles?,[2]" Yebio asked his oldest brother[3] Dan. "The pictures I've saw[4] show electrons as tiny,[5] black balls travelling around the nucleus of an atom as[6] marbles. How exciting can that be?"

"Electrons do more than act like particles," Dan replied. "Scientists have found that electrons sometimes act like waves! Imagine vibrations of energy like clouds around the nuculus[7]."

"Okay, I can except[8] that," said Yebio[9] "but what did an atom ever do for me?"

"Well, if it weren't for atoms, you couldn't see," he said, "because light is created by the processes within the atom."

Yebio was starting to get interest[10]. "What does an atom have to do [11]give off light?"

Dan thought for a moment. "I'll give you a clue. Electrons are at different energy levels as they change relationship to the nucleus. When an electron moves from lower energy to higher energy, light is absorbed. In other words, as it moves outward from the nucleus, the electron gains energy.[12]

Yebio digested the information and replied, "Then I guess light must be given off when an electron moves [13]away from[13] the nucleus."

"Exactly! An electron moving to a position of lower energy releases light."

Yebio was fully intrieged[14] with the concept. "Well, from my position," he retorted, "I'm beginning to 'see the light![15]"

1. *"What's*—Punctuation: apostrophe used with contraction **[5.1]**
2. *particles?"* —Punctuation: avoid multiple punctuation **[5.73]**
3. *brother,* Dan—Punctuation: comma used with nonessential appositive

(there can be no other *oldest* brother, so *Dan* is nonessential) **[5.29]**
4. *seen*—Grammar: past participle used in present perfect tense **[3.29. 3.36]**
5. *tiny* black—Punctuation: comma unnecessary between noncoordinate adjectives **[5.41 c]**
6. *like* marbles—Usage: word pair (like/as) **[4.18]**
7. *nucleus*—Spelling **[6.7]**
8. *accept*—Usage: word pair (except/accept) **[4.18]**
9. *Yebio,* "but—Punctuation: comma separates quote from speaker **[5.39]**
10. *interested*—Grammar: verbal (participle used as adjective) **[3.37]**
11. *to* give—Grammar: verbal (infinitive used as adverb) **[3.39]**
12. *energy."*—Punctuation: quotation marks enclose a direct quote **[5.60]**
13. *toward*—Content: see diagram and text in illustration **[2.1]**
14. *intrigued*—Spelling **[6.7]**
15. *'see the light!'"*—Punctuation: quotation marks denote special word usage (single quotation marks within quote) **[5.64, 5.67]**

Enlightened about Electrons Corrected

"What's the big deal about those particles?" Yebio asked his oldest brother, Dan. "The pictures I've seen show electrons as tiny black balls travelling around the nucleus of an atom like marbles. How exciting can that be?"

"Electrons do more than act like particles," Dan replied. "Scientists have found that electrons sometimes act like waves! Imagine vibrations of energy like clouds around the nucleus."

"Okay, I can accept that," said Yebio, "but what did an atom ever do for me?"

"Well, if it weren't for atoms, you couldn't see," he said, "because light is created by the processes within the atom."

Yebio was starting to get interested. "What does an atom have to do to give off light?"

Dan thought for a moment. "I'll give you a clue. Electrons are at different energy levels as they change relationship to the nucleus. When an electron moves from lower energy to higher energy, light is absorbed. In other words, as it moves outward from the nucleus, the electron gains energy."

Yebio digested the information and replied, "Then I guess light must be given off when an electron moves toward the nucleus."

"Exactly! An electron moving to a position of lower energy releases light."

Yebio was fully intrigued with the concept. "Well, from my position," he retorted, "I'm beginning to 'see the light!'"

10. Martian Canals Debunked

14 errors—2 content; 1 capitalization; 3 grammar; 4 punctuation; 5 usage

Martian Canals Debunked Errors

Before people could plain[1] see that the surface of Mars was desolate and rocky, popular belief held that the Red Planet could once have been inhibited[2] by people very much as[3] us.

In the late 1870's[4], the Italian Astronomer[5] Giovanni Schiaparelli started the controversy by announcing [6]on the surface of Mars[6] that he had observed what he thought were faint lines. He called these faint lines *canali*, which English translators mistakenly took to means[7] canals. Because [8]canals occur naturally and channels are manmade[8], evidence of canals on Mars would suggest a[9] advanced civilization.

American astronomer Percival Lowell popularized this belief in Martian canals in the early part of the 20th century by claiming to have affective[10] evidence of the presence of underground[11] canals on Mars. Indeed, Lowell published three books trying to convince others of the existence of canals[12] only when astronomers had telescopes powerful enough to prove that

the "canals" were really channels,[13] did the *canali* clamor subside. Nevertheless, the debate over life on Mars rage[14] on.

1. *plainly*—Grammar: adverb modifies verb **[3.4]**
2. *inhabited*—Usage: word pair (inhabited/inhibited) **[4.18]**
3. *like*—Usage: word pair (like/as) **[4.18]**
4. *1870s*—Punctuation: unnecessary apostrophe **[5.2]**
5. *astronomer*—Capital: unnecessary (not used as proper name) **[1.4]**
6. *announcing that he had observed what he thought were faint lines on the surface of Mars*—Usage: misplaced modifier **[4.15]**
7. *to mean*—Grammar: infinitive **[3.39]**
8. *canals are manmade and channels occur naturally*—Content: see caption **[2.1]**
9. *an*—Grammar: article *an* before vowel sound (an/advanced) **[3.5]**
10. *effective*—Usage: word pair (affective/ effective) **[4.18]**
11. *above-ground*—Content: see illustration **[2.1]**
12. *canals. Only*—Punctuation: run-on sentence **[5.81]**
13. *channels did*—Punctuation: comma unnecessary after introductory clause immediately preceding main verb **[5.41 d]**
14. *rages*—Usage: agreement of verb with subject (debate/rages) **[4.3]**

Martian Canals Debunked Corrected

Before people could plainly see that the surface of Mars was desolate and rocky, popular belief held that the Red Planet could once have been inhabited by people very much like us.

In the late 1870s, the Italian astronomer Giovanni Schiaparelli started the controversy by announcing that he had observed what he thought were faint lines on the surface of Mars. He called these faint lines *canali*, which English translators mistakenly took to mean canals.

Because canals are manmade and channels occur naturally, evidence of canals on Mars would suggest an advanced civilization.

American astronomer Percival Lowell popularized this belief in Martian canals in the early part of the 20th century by claiming to have effective evidence of the presence of above-ground canals on Mars. Indeed, Lowell published three books trying to convince others of the existence of canals. Only when astronomers had telescopes powerful enough to prove that the "canals" were really channels did the canali clamor subside. Nevertheless, the debate over life on Mars rages on.

11. X Marks the Spot

16 errors—1 content; 1 capitalization; 5 grammar; 7 punctuation; 1 spelling; 1 usage

X Marks the Spot Errors

Fred clambered along the steep[1] rocky hillside[2] slipping and sliding in the mud. Torrential rains from winter's[3] angry outburst had loosened the soil, and mudslides had altered the banks above the river. The *X* indicated an area below where the river forked, but it was impossible to pinpoint exactly where along the western[4] fork of the river this spot was. Suddenly[5] the ground gave way. He grabbed a nearby fern to keep from falling,[6] but succeeded only in uprooting the plant as he fell. He slid and rolled down the steep slope, landing at the base of the hill.

As he struggled to his feet, muddied and bruised, he notices[7] an opening among[8] two large rocks. He pulled out his flashlight and peered closer. A sudden glimmer caught his eye. He put the flashlight back on his belt and pulled away rocks and debris from the opening until he was able to wedge himself through. He found him[9] in what seemed to be a cave. As his eyes adjusted to the darkness, he felt around for his flashlight, which had

fallen from his belt. He quickly found it. As he picked it up, his fingers brushed against something hard, cold, and distinctly bony—something dead. Swinging it[10] around, he saw the golden light that had previously caught his eye. Propped against the wall was a cobweb-covered skeleton, and around it's[11] neck,[12] hanged[13] a golden medallion. The medallion looked just like one he had seen in a painting of the infamous pirate,[14] Varnet. Had he discovered the last resting place of this notorious brigand? "Well, yo ho ho," he sang, [15]and a bag full of gold. I'll be rich!" Could anyone be as lucky as him[16]?

1. *steep, rocky*—Punctuation: comma separates coordinate adjectives **[5.24]**
2. *hillside, slipping*—Punctuation: comma used to avoid ambiguity (terminal participle) **[5.36]**
3. *Winter's*—Capital: season personified **[1.12]**
4. *eastern*—Content: see illustration **[2.1]** (Acceptable: *southeastern*)
5. *Suddenly,*—Punctuation: comma used after introductory word **[5.25]**
6. *falling but*—Punctuation: comma unnecessary in compound predicate **[5.41 h]**
7. *noticed*—Grammar: past tense verb **[3.29]**
8. *between*—Usage: word pair (among/between) **[4.18]**
9. found *himself*—Grammar: reflexive pronoun **[3.25]**
10. *his flashlight*—Grammar: ambiguous pronoun reference **[3.19]**
11. *its*—Spelling (or Punctuation: apostrophe unnecessary) **[5.1, 6.1]**
12. *neck hung*—Punctuation: comma unnecessary after dependent phrase immediately preceding main verb **[5.41 d]**
13. *hung*—Grammar: past tense verb **[3.27, 3.29]**
14. *pirate* Varnet—Punctuation: comma unnecessary with essential appositive **[5.41 i]**

15. *"and*—Punctuation: quotation marks enclose both parts of divided quotation **[5.60]**

16. *he*—Grammar: pronoun following *as* in incomplete construction **[3.24]**

X Marks the Spot Corrected

Fred clambered along the steep, rocky hillside, slipping and sliding in the mud. Torrential rains from Winter's angry outburst had loosened the soil, and mudslides had altered the banks above the river. The *X* indicated an area below where the river forked, but it was impossible to pinpoint exactly where along the eastern fork of the river this spot was. Suddenly, the ground gave way. He grabbed a nearby fern to keep from falling but succeeded only in uprooting the plant as he fell. He slid and rolled down the steep slope, landing at the base of the hill.

As he struggled to his feet, muddied and bruised, he noticed an opening between two large rocks. He pulled out his flashlight and peered closer. A sudden glimmer caught his eye. He put the flashlight back on his belt and pulled away rocks and debris from the opening until he was able to wedge himself through. He found himself in what seemed to be a cave. As his eyes adjusted to the darkness, he felt around for his flashlight, which had fallen from his belt. He quickly found it. As he picked it up, his fingers brushed against something hard, cold, and distinctly bony—something dead. Swinging his flashlight around, he saw the golden light that had previously caught his eye. Propped against the wall was a cobweb-covered skeleton, and around its neck hung a golden medallion. The medallion looked just like one he had seen in a painting of the infamous pirate Varnet. Had he discovered the last resting place of this notorious brigand? "Well, yo ho ho," he sang, "and a bag full of gold. I'll be rich!" Could anyone be as lucky as he?

12. Musical Tic-Tac-Toe

14 errors—3 content; 1 grammar; 6 punctuation; 1 spelling; 3 usage

Musical Tic-Tac-Toe Errors

"Welcome to Musical Tic-Tac-Toe. Todays[1] theme is composers. Behind each treble clef is a picture of a composer. Each time a player chooses a square, [2]they are[2] flipped. A correct identification gains the player an outlined picture[3] an incorrect answer means the picture is flipped back over. Get any three in a row to win.

"Let's get to it. Player One, you've chosen to start in the center. Here's your clue: This German composer wrote nine symphonys[4], but the first four notes of his Symphony No. 5 are possibly the most recognized in the world. Who is he?[5]

"He is Beethoven."

"Ludwig van Beethoven is correct. The center picture is now outlined in black. Player Two chooses the top left square. This Austrian composer wrote more than 100 symphonies and was referred to even by his contemporaries as 'Papa'."[6]

"That would be Haydn."

"Franz Joseph Haydn is correct. Your picture is outlined in gray[7], and you've blocked your opponent. Player One wants the top middle square. This American become[8] known as the father of ragtime."

"I'll say Joplin."

"Scott Joplin is correct. Player Two has now chosen the bottom middle square. This German's works [9]both include[9] operas and orchestral pieces, but he is most famous for his oratorio *Messiah*."

"Is it Chopin[10]?"

"Correct. You've got another block. Yes, Player One, you can[11] have the top right square. This Austrian started composing at age five. He is famous for the opera *The Magic Flute*. Who is he"?[12]

"He is Mozart."

"Wolfgang Amadeus Mozart is correct. Player Two, which space would you like?

To the bottom right[13] we go. This Italian composer is famous for his operas, including *Rigoletto* and *Aida*. Who is he?"

"I'd say it's Puccini."

"No. Player One[14] do you know?"

"Yes. It's Verdi."

"Giuseppe Verdi is right. You've won!"

1. *Today's*—Punctuation: 's used with singular possessive **[5.4]**
2. *it is*—Usage: agreement of noun and verb with possessive pronoun in number **[4.2, 4.3]**
3. *picture;*—Punctuation: semicolon separates main clauses joined without coordinating conjunction **[5.68]**
4. *symphonies*—Spelling **[6.4]**
5. *he?"*—Punctuation: quotation marks after final paragraph of quote spanning several paragraphs **[5.62]**
6. *'Papa.'"*—Punctuation: period inside quotation marks (both sets) **[5.54]**
7. *white*—Content: see illustration and caption **[2.1]**
8. *became*—Grammar: past tense (irregular) **[3.29]**
9. *include both*—Usage: correlative conjunctions (*both / and*) each followed by parallel phrase **[4.13]**
10. *Handel*—Content: see caption **[2.1]**
11. *may*—Usage: word pair (can/may) **[4.18]**
12. *he?"*—Punctuation: question mark inside quotation marks when it applies to quoted material **[5.58]**
13. *left*—Content: see illustration **[2.1]**
14. *One,*—Punctuation: comma used with noun of address **[5.27]**

Musical Tic-Tac-Toe Corrected

"Welcome to Musical Tic-Tac-Toe. Today's theme is composers. Behind each treble clef is a picture of a composer. Each time a player chooses a square, it is flipped. A correct identification gains the player an outlined picture; an incorrect answer means the picture is flipped back over. Get any three in a row to win.

"Let's get to it. Player One, you've chosen to start in the center. Here's your clue: This German composer wrote nine symphonies, but the first four notes of his Symphony No. 5 are possibly the most recognized in the world. Who is he?"

"He is Beethoven."

"Ludwig van Beethoven is correct. The center picture is now outlined in black. Player Two chooses the top left square. This Austrian composer wrote more than 100 symphonies and was referred to even by his contemporaries as 'Papa.'"

"That would be Haydn."

"Franz Joseph Haydn is correct. Your picture is outlined in white, and you've blocked your opponent. Player One wants the top middle square. This American became known as the father of ragtime."

"I'll say Joplin."

"Scott Joplin is correct. Player Two has now chosen the bottom middle square. This German's works include both operas and orchestral pieces, but he is most famous for his oratorio *Messiah*."

"Is it Handel?"

"Correct. You've got another block. Yes, Player One, you can have the top right square. This Austrian started composing at age five. He is famous for the opera *The Magic Flute*. Who is he?"

"He is Mozart."

"Wolfgang Amadeus Mozart is correct. Player Two, which space would you like? To the bottom left we go. This Italian composer is famous for his operas, including *Rigoletto* and *Aida*. Who is he?"

"I'd say it's Puccini."

"No. Player One, do you know?"

"Yes. It's Verdi."

"Giuseppe Verdi is right. You've won!"

13.   Easter Island Mystery

16 errors—1 content; 2 capitalization; 1 grammar; 5 punctuation; 7 usage

Easter Island Mystery Errors

On Easter of 1722, a Dutch admiral named Jacob Roggeveen discovered the small polynesian[1] island he later named Easter Island. Nearing the shore, admiral[2] Roggeveen was astounded to see [3]huge stone figures on raised platforms with long ears[3].

The island was peopled by two distinct groups: those who had long ears (stretched to hold wooden plugs) and [4]regular-eared people[4]. With this revelation, visitors to the island was[5] able to imply[6] that the statues had been made by the [7]long eared[7] people.

There has been much conjecture about the method used to raise these huge monuments from their prone positions. The islanders had no heavy wood with which to create lifting equipment, yet they had[8] able to erect hard-lava sculptures weighing up to 50 tons and standing as tall as 40[9] feet. In 1956, Thor Heyerdahl, Norwegian archaeologist, enlisted twelve island men to show how the objects could have been lifted. Though it took 18 days[10] the men raised a 20-ton statue from where it lied[11,12] using only muscles, poles, and stones.

An even bigger mystery has been the means of transporting statues from the quarry to the display platforms. Asked to reveal the secret, islanders insisted that the statues had walked under their own power[13] not by someone elses[14]! Some researchers, however, came up with the explanation that the statues could of[15] been rocked, side to side, while being pulled by rope (similar to the way in which we might move an upright refrigerator). The affect[16] would have been that the statues appeared, from a distance, to be walking!

However these unusual statues came to stand guard on Easter Island, they provide a tantalizing mystery to students, researchers, and other inquiring minds.

1. *Polynesian*—Capital: proper adjective **[1.5]**
2. *Admiral*—Capital: title used as part of name **[1.8]**
3. *huge, long-eared stone figures on raised platforms*—Usage: misplaced modifier **[4.15]**
4. *those who had regular ears*—Usage: parallel construction **[4.12]**
5. *were*—Usage: agreement of verb with subject separated **[4.3]**
6. *infer*—Usage: word pair (infer/imply) **[4.18]**
7. *long-eared*—Punctuation: hyphen used in compound adjective **[5.48]**
8. had *been* able—Grammar: past participle (used in past perfect tense) **[3.29, 3.36]** (Acceptable: *were able*)
9. *30*—Content: see caption **[2.1]**
10. *days,*—Punctuation: comma used after introductory dependent clause **[5.26]**
11. *lay*—Usage: (past tense of *lie*) word pair (lie/lay) **[4.18]**
12. *lay, using*—Punctuation: comma used to avoid ambiguity **[5.36]**
13. *power,*—Punctuation: comma used with contrasting expressions **[5.34]**
14. *else's*—Punctuation: 's used with possessive indefinite pronoun **[5.7]**
15. *could have*—Usage: word pair (of/have) **[4.18]**
16. *effect*—Usage: word pair (affect/effect) **[4.18]**

Easter Island Mystery Corrected

On Easter of 1722, a Dutch admiral named Jacob Roggeveen discovered the small Polynesian island he later named Easter Island. Nearing the shore, Admiral Roggeveen was astounded to see huge, long-eared stone figures on raised platforms.

The island was peopled by two distinct groups: those who had long ears (stretched to hold wooden plugs) and those who had regular ears. With this revelation, visitors to the island were able to infer that the statues had been made by the long-eared people.

There has been much conjecture about the method used to raise these huge monuments from their prone positions.

The islanders had no heavy wood with which to create lifting equipment, yet they had been able to erect hard-lava sculptures weighing up to 50 tons and standing as tall as 30 feet. In 1956, Thor Heyerdahl, Norwegian archaeologist, enlisted twelve island men to show how the objects could have been lifted. Though it took 18 days, the men raised a 20-ton statue from where it lay, using only muscles, poles, and stones.

An even bigger mystery has been the means of transporting statues from the quarry to the display platforms. Asked to reveal the secret, islanders insisted that the statues had walked under their own power, not by someone else's! Some researchers, however, came up with the explanation that the statues could have been rocked, side to side, while being pulled by rope (similar to the way in which we might move an upright refrigerator). The effect would have been that the statues appeared, from a distance, to be walking!

However these unusual statues came to stand guard on Easter Island, they provide a tantalizing mystery to students, researchers, and other inquiring minds.

14. Kindergarten Woes

15 errors—1 content; 2 capitalization; 1 grammar; 8 punctuation; 2 spelling; 1 usage

Kindergarten Woes Errors

Alan pondered for a moment before beginning his analysis. He would have to write speedily in order to finish.

In Ernest Hemingway's short story "A Clean, Well-Lighted place[1]"[2] the character of the old man is seen through the eyes of two men whom Hemingway simply chooses to call "the older waiter" and "the younger waiter." A contrast is established not only between youth and old age but also between the [3]empathy of the younger waiter and the intolerance of the older[3] waiter. The younger waiter sees nothing

but a nasty old man which[4] is keeping him from his wife and home. To the younger waiter, the old man is just another drunk who should move on. [5]An impression that is made clear when he complains to the older waiter, "Hombre, there are bodegas open all night long." The younger waiter does not understand what it is like to be alone in the world. He has youth, a family to go home to, a future, and hope. He boasts, "I am confidence. I am all confidence"[6] The older waiter, however, sees a very different man. He sees a clean man who drinks without spilling. He sees a man who once had a wife: a man who, like himself, needs the semblance of normalcy that he finds in the clean, well-lighted cafe,[7] the cafe, unlike the bodega, is a place where decency and order can be found.

"Boys and girls," Mrs. Crabtree interrupted, [8]snack time is over. [9]find your places on the floor, and cross your hands[10], and legs."

"If only I was[11] a little older," Alan sighed, "I could rid myself of these silly little snack breaks. When will I ever finish this analyses[12]![13]Did Poe or Einstein have to stop when snack break ended or sit with his hands and legs crossed?![14] The injustices of kindergarten is[15] vast."

1. *Place*—Capital: title of story **[1.14]**
2. *Place,"*—Punctuation: comma used inside quotation marks **[5.40]**
3. *intolerance of the younger...empathy of the older*—Content: see caption **[2.1]** (Acceptable: *empathy of the older...intolerance of the younger*)
4. *who*—Usage: agreement of pronoun with noun **[4.2]** (Acceptable: *that* or *, who*)
5. *on, an*—Punctuation: sentence fragment **[5.82]**
6. *confidence."*—Punctuation: period inside quotation marks **[5.54]**
7. *cafe. The*—Punctuation: period corrects comma splice **[5.81]**
8. *"snack*—Punctuation: quotation marks enclose both parts of divided quotation **[5.60]**

9. *Find*—Capital: first word in a sentence **[1.1]**

10. *hands and legs*—Punctuation: comma unnecessary in compound object **[5.41 m]**

11. *were*—Grammar: subjunctive mood used in contrary-to-fact statement **[3.32]**

12. *analysis*—Spelling **[6.5]**

13. *analysis?*—Punctuation: question mark after direct question **[5.56]**

14. *crossed?*—Punctuation: avoid multiple punctuation **[5.73]**

15. *are*—Usage: agreement of verb with subject (separated) **[4.3]**

Kindergarten Woes Corrected

Alan pondered for a moment before beginning his analysis. He would have to write speedily in order to finish.

In Ernest Hemingway's short story "A Clean, Well-Lighted Place," the character of the old man is seen through the eyes of two men whom Hemingway simply chooses to call "the older waiter" and "the younger waiter." A contrast is established not only between youth and old age but also between the empathy of the older waiter and the intolerance of the younger waiter. The younger waiter sees nothing but a nasty old man who is keeping him from his wife and home. To the younger waiter, the old man is just another drunk who should move on, an impression that is made clear when he complains to the older waiter, "Hombre, there are bodegas open all night long." The younger waiter does not understand what it is like to be alone in the world. He has youth, a family to go home to, a future, and hope. He boasts, "I am confidence. I am all confidence." The older waiter, however, sees a very different man. He sees a clean man who drinks without spilling. He sees a man who once had a wife: a man who, like himself, needs the semblance of normalcy that he finds in the clean, well-lighted cafe. The cafe, unlike the bodega, is a place where decency and order can be found.

"Boys and girls," Mrs. Crabtree interrupted, "snack time is over. Find your places on the floor and cross your hands and legs."

"If only I were a little older," Alan sighed, "I could rid myself of these silly little snack breaks. When will I ever finish this analysis? Did Poe or Einstein have to stop when snack break ended or sit with his hands and legs crossed? The injustices of kindergarten are vast."

15. A Questionable Bargain

16 errors—1 content; 11 punctuation; 4 usage

A Questionable Bargain Errors

1662 Camino Sierra
Bakersfield[1] CA 93306
March 11, 1999

Danson's Deals (D.D.)
Customer Service Department
P.O. Box 11196
Houston, TX 77111

To whom it may concern,[2]

Enclosed you will find several items that I am returning;[3] one pair of clogs, [4]$37, one skirt, $29, a child's dress and hat, $15, and a child's T-shirt, $9[4]. On February 19, 1999[5] I spoke to Madeline Gonzales[6] Director of Customer Service at D.D.'s main office in Tulsa, Okla. She told me that, although I did not have a receipt, I could return the items[7]. If[7] there were manufacturer's defects or other problems.

At the time I made the purchase, I thought the deals were "too good to be true;[8]" after receiving the items, I realized I was right. The skirt was missing a button, the T-shirt turned an entire load of wash pink, and the dress and matching hat was[9] stained. In addition, the clogs were two different sizes: neither were[10] the size six,[11] that I ordered.

[12]Either I would like[12] a complete refund of my money or store credit for the total (price + tax = $96.30[13].[14]) Included in

the envelope is[15] my account number and credit card number.

I look forward to your prompt reply.

Sincerely[16]
Mei Lee
Mei Lee

1. *Bakersfield,* CA—Punctuation: comma separates elements of address **[5.15]**
2. *concern:*—Punctuation: colon used after greeting of a business letter **[5.9]**
3. *returning:*—Punctuation: colon introduces a list of items **[5.10]**
4. *$37; one skirt, $29; a child's dress and hat, $15; and a child's T-shirt, $9.*—Punctuation: semicolon separates items (in a series) containing commas **[5.70]**
5. *1999,*—Punctuation: comma used after year in sentence **[5.18]**
6. *Madeline Gonzales,*—Punctuation: comma separates name and title **[5.20]**
7. *items if*—Punctuation: sentence fragment **[5.82]**
8. *true";*—Punctuation: semicolon outside quotation mark **[5.72]**
9. *were*—Usage: agreement of verb with compound subject joined by *and* **[4.6]**
10. *neither was*—Usage: agreement of verb with indefinite pronoun **[4.8]**
11. *six* that—Punctuation: comma unnecessary with essential clause **[5.41 i]**
12. *I would like either*—Usage: correlative conjunctions (either/or) each followed by parallel phrase **[4.13]**
13. *$97.20*—Content: see caption and illustration ($90 + 8% sales tax = $97.20) **[2.1]**
14. *$97.20).*—Punctuation: period outside parenthesis **[5.55]**
15. are—Usage: agreement of verb with subject (when verb is placed before subject) **[4.3]**
16. Sincerely,—Punctuation: comma used after closing of letter **[5.21]**

A Questionable Bargain Corrected

1662 Camino Sierra
Bakersfield, CA 93306
March 11, 1999

Danson's Deals (D.D.)
Customer Service Department
P.O. Box 11196
Houston, TX 77111

To whom it may concern:

Enclosed you will find several items that I am returning: one pair of clogs, $37; one skirt, $29; a child's dress and hat, $15; and a child's T-shirt, $9. On February 19, 1999, I spoke to Madeline Gonzales, Director of Customer Service at D.D.'s main office in Tulsa, Okla. She told me that, although I did not have a receipt, I could return the items if there were manufacturer's defects or other problems.

At the time I made the purchase, I thought the deals were "too good to be true"; after receiving the items, I realized I was right. The skirt was missing a button, the T-shirt turned an entire load of wash pink, and the dress and matching hat were stained. In addition, the clogs were two different sizes: neither was the size six that I ordered.

I would like either a complete refund of my money or store credit for the total (price + tax = 97.20). Included in the envelope are my account number and credit card number.

I look forward to your prompt reply.

Sincerely,
Mei Lee
Mei Lee

16. The Watergate Scandal

15 errors—3 content; 1 capitalization; 1 grammar; 9 punctuation; 1 usage

The Watergate Scandal Errors

The Watergate investigation uncovered

one of the biggest political scandals in United States history.

In June,[1] 1972, five men hired by the Republican Party's Committee for the Re-election of the President (C.R.P.) were arrested for breaking into the Democratic Party's national headquarters. The men were charged with several crimes, includ-ing:[2] burglary and wiretapping. President Richard Nixon immediately directed White House Counsel John Dean to begin a coverup. Accusations that any White House official had been involved,[3] were repeatedly denied, although reports to the contrary were soon uncovered by the media.

The Senate Select Committee on Presi-dential Campaign Activities were[4] orga-nized to investigate the affair in February 1973. Shortly after that, Nixon accepted the resignations of several of his Advisors[5] (including John Dean)[6] however, Nixon continued to deny it[7].

In May 1973, the committee began hearings on the Watergate matter. John Dean accused the President of a coverup. Three[8] months later, the committee learned that Nixon had in his office a recording system,[9] that he had used to tape conversations. Select tapes were promptly subpoenaed[10] but Nixon refused to turn them over, claiming it was his executive privilege to keep the tapes. The Supreme Court voted unanimously that the tapes were not covered by executive privilege,[11] eight hours after the judgment, Nixon released the tapes.

A formal impeachment inquiry began in May 1973[12]. Two months later, the House Judiciary Committee recommended four[13] articles of impeachment. In August, Nixon released additional transcripts of tapes,[14] that clearly implicated him in the coverup [15]and with his credibility badly damaged in Congress, Nixon announced his resignation and became the first Presi-dent of the United States to resign from office.

1. *June 1972* — Punctuation: comma unnecessary between month and year **[5.41 a]**
2. *including burglary* — Punctuation: colon unnecessary **[5.13]**
3. *involved were* — Punctuation: comma unnecessary before verb **[5.41 e]**
4. *was* — Usage: agreement of verb with collective subject used in singular sense (committee/was) **[4.4]**
5. *advisors* — Capital: unnecessary (title not used as part of name) **[1.8]**
6. *Dean); however* — Punctuation: semico-lon used before conjunctive adverb joining independent clauses **[5.69]**
7. *that any White House official had been involved* — Grammar: ambiguous pronoun reference (Accept any reason-ably worded answer with similar meaning.) **[3.19]**
8. *Two* months — Content: see illustration **[2.1]**
9. *system* that — Punctuation: comma unnecessary with essential clause **[5.41 i]**
10. *subpoenaed, but* — Punctuation: comma used before coordinating conjunction joining independent clauses **[5.37]**
11. *privilege;* — Punctuation: semicolon separates main clauses joined without coordinating conjunction (corrects comma splice) **[5.68]**
12. *1974* — Content: see illustration **[2.1]**
13. *three* — Content: see illustration **[2.1]**
14. *tapes that* — Punctuation: comma unnecessary with essential phrase **[5.41 i]**
15. *coverup. With* — Punctuation: run-on sentence **[5.81]**

The Watergate Scandal Corrected

The Watergate investigation uncovered one of the biggest political scandals in United States history.

In June 1972, five men hired by the Republican Party's Committee for the Re-election of the President (C.R.P.) were arrested for breaking into the Democratic Party's national headquarters. The men were charged with several crimes, including burglary and wiretapping. President Richard Nixon immediately directed White House Counsel John Dean to begin a coverup. Accusations that any White House official had been involved were repeatedly denied, although reports to the contrary were soon uncovered by the media.

The Senate Select Committee on Presidential Campaign Activities was organized to investigate the affair in February 1973. Shortly after that, Nixon accepted the resignations of several of his advisors (including John Dean); however, Nixon continued to deny that any White House official had been involved.

In May 1973, the committee began hearings on the Watergate matter. John Dean accused the President of a coverup. Two months later, the committee learned that Nixon had in his office a recording system that he had used to tape conversations. Select tapes were promptly subpoenaed, but Nixon refused to turn them over, claiming it was his executive privilege to keep the tapes. The Supreme Court voted unanimously that the tapes were not covered by executive privilege; eight hours after the judgment, Nixon released the tapes.

A formal impeachment inquiry began in May 1974. Two months later, the House Judiciary Committee recommended three articles of impeachment. In August, Nixon released additional transcripts of tapes that clearly implicated him in the coverup. With his credibility badly damaged in Congress, Nixon announced his resignation and became the first President of the United States to resign from office.

17. Getting in Sync

18 errors—2 content; 1 capitalization; 6 grammar; 3 punctuation; 6 usage

Getting in Sync Errors

Jogging past the womens'[1] dormitory of her new college, Melody Horn was feeling "jazzed;[2]" she fell into a rhythm with another runner who didn't seem as anxious[3] to start school.

"If I [4]would only have learned to schedule my time during the first year," Ann Holtzmann complained, "I [5]will have[5] gotten some [6]Bs and maybe an A or two. I wouldn't have fallen flat!"

"You can't beat time management. They really drummed it in at my high school—my whole class improved its[7] grades. Now, though, I have to pick my classes and learn to study in a new place. These kind[8] of responsibilities are tough."

"You sound pretty sharp," Ann noted. "What do you want to do here?"

"I have a natural inclination for music, so I'll study that as my major. I need Music Theory I, and I must choose among[9] the other two music classes offered to freshmen. I just hope I get flexible teachers."

"Not all the staff is[10] the same, so don't leave it to chance. If I was[11] you, I'd take Sak for Music Theory I. Make a note of it!"

"Oh, no! Taking Sak would mean a Friday[12] class. Well, that's a minor concern if she's well[13] at teaching. Anyway, given[14] up Ono's section one will free me to take the section three techniques class from Oz[15]. Let's see, for general education I'll take an English writing course and a History[16] class. Algebra or a general math class are[17] required, so I'm hoping to take the Math for Musicians class. I'll schedule my assignment and practice times around all my classes."

"By the time you start second semester, you will already take[18] most of your freshman requirements! I think I'll sign up for time management!" Ann yelled, heading for the locker room.

Melody continued her run solo, glad that Ann was singing a new tune.

1. *women's*—Punctuation: *'s* used with possessive of plural not ending in *s* **[5.6]**

2. *jazzed";*—Punctuation: semicolon outside quotation marks **[5.72]**

3. *eager*—Usage: word pair (eager/anxious) **[4.18]**

4. *had only*—Grammar: avoid *would have* in *if* clause (use past perfect tense) **[3.31]**

5. *would have*—Grammar: subjunctive mood used in contrary-to-fact statement **[3.32]**

6. *B's*—Punctuation: apostrophe used with plural of letter **[5.2]**

7. *their*—Usage: agreement of possessive pronoun with collective subject used in the plural sense **[4.5]**

8. *kinds*—Usage: agreement of adjective with noun (these/kinds) **[4.10]**

9. *between*—Usage: word pair (among/ between) **[4.18]**

10. *are*—Usage: agreement of verb with collective subject used in a plural sense **[4.4]**

11. *were*—Grammar: subjunctive mood used in contrary-to-fact statement **[3.32]**

12. *Saturday*—Content: see illustration **[2.1]**

13. *good*—Grammar: adjective modifies noun **[3.1]**

14. *giving*—Grammar: verbal (gerund) **[3.38]**

15. *Gold*—Content: see illustration **[2.1]**

16. *history*—Capital: unnecessary (not used as proper noun) **[1.4]**

17. *is*—Usage: agreement of verb with closer of two subjects joined by *or* **[4.6]**

18. *have taken*—Grammar: context of article requires future perfect tense **[3.29]**

Getting in Sync Corrected

Jogging past the women's dormitory of her new college, Melody Horn was feeling "jazzed"; she fell into a rhythm with an-other runner who didn't seem as eager to start school.

"If I had only learned to schedule my time during the first year," Ann Holtzmann complained, "I would have gotten some B's and maybe an A or two. I wouldn't have fallen flat!"

"You can't beat time management. They really drummed it in at my high school—my whole class improved their grades. Now, though, I have to pick my classes and learn to study in a new place. These kinds of responsibilities are tough."

"You sound pretty sharp," Ann noted. "What do you want to do here?"

"I have a natural inclination for music, so I'll study that as my major. I need Music Theory I, and I must choose be-tween the other two music classes offered to freshmen. I just hope I get flexible teachers."

"Not all the staff are the same, so don't leave it to chance. If I were you, I'd take Sak for Music Theory I. Make a note of it!"

"Oh, no! Taking Sak would mean a Saturday class. Well, that's a minor con-cern if she's good at teaching. Anyway, giving up Ono's section one will free me to take the section three techniques class from Gold. Let's see, for general education I'll take an English writing course and a history class. Algebra or a general math class is required, so I'm hoping to take the Math for Musicians class. I'll schedule my assignment and practice times around all my classes."

"By the time you start second semes-ter, you will already have taken most of your freshman requirements! I think I'll sign up for time management!" Ann yelled, heading for the locker room.

Melody continued her run solo, glad that Ann was singing a new tune.

18. A Question of Gravity

18 errors—2 content; 3 grammar; 7 punctuation; 4 spelling; 2 usage

A Question of Gravity Errors

"Aristotle, famed scientist and philosopher, argued that heavy objects fall faster than light objects. Mathematician, astronomer, and [1]physicist, Galileo,[1] stated that light and heavy objects fall at the same rate. Who was right? Today, I will test these theories and let you, my fellow classmates, see who's[2] theory is correct."[3]

"I have in my hands two objects: a hardball and a pingpong ball. [4]If dropped at the same time, how many of you think the hardball will hit the floor first?"[4] Jarrod asked his captive audience. "How many of you think the balls will hit at the same time?" Jarrod recorded the results on the chalkboard,[5] alot[6] more students agreed with Aristotle[7]. "I will now drop both objects at the same time and from the same height. I want you [8]to closely watch[8]"![9] Jarrod dropped the objects. As the majority of the class had anticipated, the balls hit the ground at [10]different times[10]. "Very good, you've been as studious as me[11]. Alright[12], I have one more experiment to perform. This should be a piece of cake for smart students like ourselves[13]."

Jarrod pulled out two pieces of paper from his binder and crumpled one of them up. "How many of you think these two pieces of paper will hit at the same time?".[14] A few students agreed that both pieces of paper would hit at the same time. Several more were undecided. "I am holding both papers at the same height, and I am now dropping it[15] at the same time." The crumpled paper landed first. "I ask you now[16] Was Galileo right only some of the time? Is gravity not constant?" Jarrod paused momentarily. "Yes, gravity is constant! What you have witnessed here is air resistance. The flat[17] unaltered sheet has more air resistance than the crumpled sheet of paper, so it falls more slowly. Galileo's law of falling objects, therefore, can be proven only when there is no air resistance."

The class applauded. Jarrod's demonstration was sure to recieve[18] high marks.

1. *physicist Galileo* — Punctuation: commas unnecessary with essential appositive [5.41 i]
2. *whose* — Spelling [6.1]
3. *correct.* — Punctuation: quotation marks unnecessary at end of paragraph (except last) for quote spanning several paragraphs [5.62]
4. *If the balls are dropped...* — Usage: dangling modifier [4.16] (Acceptable: *If dropped at the same time, which ball will hit the floor first?*, etc.)
5. *chalkboard; a lot* — Punctuation: semicolon separates main clauses joined without coordinating conjunction (corrects comma splice) [5.68] (Acceptable: chalkboard. A lot...)
6. *a lot* — Spelling [6.6]
7. *Galileo* — Content: see illustration [2.1]
8. *to watch closely* — Grammar: don't split infinitive [3.40]
9. *closely!"* — Punctuation: exclamation point inside quotation marks [5.44]
10. *the same time* — Content: see caption [2.1]
11. *I* — Grammar: pronoun following *as* in incomplete construction [3.24]
12. *All right* — Spelling [6.6]
13. students like *us* — Grammar: pronoun used as object (objective case instead of reflexive) [3.22]
14. *time?* — Punctuation: avoid multiple punctuation [5.73]
15. *them* — Usage: agreement of pronoun with subject [4.2]
16. *now, Was* — Punctuation: comma introduces direct question within sentence [5.35]
17. *flat, unaltered* — Punctuation: comma separates coordinate adjectives [5.24]
18. *receive* — Spelling [6.7]

A Question of Gravity Corrected

"Aristotle, famed scientist and philosopher, argued that heavy objects fall faster than light objects. Mathematician, astronomer, and physicist Galileo stated that light and heavy objects fall at the same rate. Who was right? Today, I will test these theories and let you, my fellow classmates, see whose theory is correct.

"I have in my hands two objects: a hardball and a pingpong ball. If the balls are dropped at the same time, how many of you think the hardball will hit the floor first?" Jarrod asked his captive audience. "How many of you think the balls will hit at the same time?" Jarrod recorded the results on the chalkboard; a lot more students agreed with Galileo. "I will now drop both objects at the same time and from the same height. I want you to watch closely!" Jarrod dropped the objects. As the majority of the class had anticipated, the balls hit the ground at the same time. "Very good, you've been as studious as I. All right, I have one more experiment to perform. This should be a piece of cake for smart students like us."

Jarrod pulled out two pieces of paper from his binder and crumpled one of them up. "How many of you think these two pieces of paper will hit at the same time?" A few students agreed that both pieces of paper would hit at the same time. Several more were undecided. "I am holding both papers at the same height, and I am now dropping them at the same time." The crumpled paper landed first. "I ask you now, Was Galileo right only some of the time? Is gravity not constant?" Jarrod paused momentarily. "Yes, gravity is constant! What you have witnessed here is air resistance. The flat, unaltered sheet has more air resistance than the crumpled sheet of paper, so it falls more slowly. Galileo's law of falling objects, therefore, can be proven only when there is no air resistance."

The class applauded. Jarrod's oral demonstration was sure to receive high marks.

19. Creatures that Glow in the Dark

16 errors—2 content; 3 grammar; 8 punctuation; 3 usage

Creatures that Glow in the Dark Errors

Bioluminescence, the emission of light produced by some living organisms, is a fascinating [1]if little-known[1] subject. Fireflies are the most common example of terrestrial animals that glow in the dark[2] but the majority of luminous organisms are marine animals.[3] That lived[4] in moderate to great depths.

Bioluminescence involves light production without heat. Either an animal can be self-luminescent[5] producing its own light, or they[6] may use the light from parasitic[7] bacteria carried in its body in gland-like structures. Most animals that glow are self-luminescent, producing light by a chemical reaction. The enzyme luciferase promotes a reaction,[8] between oxygen and a substance in the organism called luciferin. It[9] usually takes place in special organs called photophores. The pattern and the amount of light can vary.

Scientists are still hypothesizing about the reasons why animals produce light?[10] Sexual attraction may be one reason; the fireflies[11] flashing abdomens attract mates. The opposing roles of predator and prey offer further possible reasons for animal bioluminescence. Some animals use light as a lure for attracting prey,[12] for example, the aptly named anglerfish has a photophore (a bulblike light organ) at the base[13] of a long, flexible rod that it can dangle in front of its mouth like a fishing line with bait. Other fish use their light displays to avoid becoming prey, using flashing light patterns [14]while they escape to distract their predators.[14] The Atlantic midshipman is a fish known to flash its light on,[15] and off at approaching predators, perhaps warning them away from its venomous spine. Another way to avoid enemies is by counterillumination. The fish matches the intensity and angle of sunlight with its own luminescence, thereby erasing its shadow.

Scientists still have a great deal to learn about bioluminescence. As exploration into the deep sea increases, they would[16] be able to learn even more about how and why so many marine animals glow in the dark.

1. *fascinating, if little-known,* subject—Punctuation: comma used with contrasting expressions [5.34]

2. *dark, but*—Punctuation: comma used before coordinating conjunction joining independent clauses [5.37]

3. *animals that*—Punctuation: sentence fragment [5.82]

4. *live*—Grammar: present tense [3.29]

5. *luminescent, producing*—Punctuation: comma used with nonessential participial phrase [5.31]

6. *it*—Usage: agreement of pronoun with noun (animal/it) [4.2]

7. *symbiotic*—Content: see caption [2.1]

8. *reaction between*—Punctuation: comma unnecessary with essential clause [5.41 i]

9. *Light production*—Grammar: ambiguous pronoun reference [3.19] (Acceptable: *The chemical reaction*)

10. *light.*—Punctuation: question mark unnecessary [5.57]

11. *fireflies'*—Punctuation: apostrophe used with possessive of plural ending in *s* [5.5]

12. *prey; for example*—Punctuation: semicolon used before conjunctive adverb joining independent clauses [5.69] (Acceptable: *prey. For*)

13. at the *tip*—Content: see illustration [2.1] (Acceptable: *end*)

14. patterns *to distract their predators while they escape.*—Usage: misplaced modifier [4.15]

15. *on and off*—Punctuation: comma unnecessary between adverbs [5.41 j]

16. *will* be able—Grammar: helping verb in future tense [3.29, 3.33]

Creatures that Glow in the Dark Corrected

Bioluminescence, the emission of light produced by some living organisms, is a fascinating, if little-known, subject. Fireflies are the most common example of terrestrial animals that glow in the dark, but the majority of luminous organisms are marine animals that live in moderate to great depths.

Bioluminescence involves light production without heat. Either an animal can be self-luminescent, producing its own light, or it may use the light from symbiotic bacteria carried in its body in gland-like structures. Most animals that glow are self-luminescent, producing light by a chemical reaction. The enzyme luciferase promotes a reaction between oxygen and a substance in the organism called luciferin. Light production usually takes place in special organs called photophores. The pattern and the amount of light can vary.

Scientists are still hypothesizing about the reasons why animals produce light. Sexual attraction may be one reason; the fireflies' flashing abdomens attract mates. The opposing roles of predator and prey offer further possible reasons for animal bioluminescence. Some animals use light as a lure for attracting prey; for example, the aptly named anglerfish has a photophore (a bulblike light organ) at the tip of a long, flexible rod that it can dangle in front of its mouth like a fishing line with bait. Other fish use their light displays to avoid becoming prey, using flashing light patterns to distract their predators while they escape. The Atlantic midshipman is a fish known to flash its light on and off at approaching predators, perhaps warning them away from its venomous spine. Another way to avoid enemies is by counterillumination. The fish matches the intensity and angle of sunlight with its own luminescence, thereby erasing its shadow.

Scientists still have a great deal to learn about bioluminescence. As exploration into the deep sea increases, they will be able to learn even more about how and why so many marine animals glow in the dark.

20. *E* for Einstein

17 errors—2 content; 1 grammar; 12 punctuation; 2 usage

E for Einstein Errors

Many of us know Albert Einstein for his equation,[1] $E = n^2c^2$ and the idea that [3]energy is simply mass[3] that is "frozen".[4] Each of us who has heard of Albert Einstein and his theories has their[5] image of Albert the genius. However, what do we know of Albert,[6] the child who became the famous man?

Albert was seen as an unpromising youth for several reasons (in fact, his success would surprise many people:[7]) his early slowness in learning, his disdain for physical activity, and his dislike of school. Albert did not learn to speak until he was three years old (not by the usual age two!)[8] He did not enjoy outdoor childrens'[9] games; he complained that strenuous,[10] physical activity made him dizzy. Instead[11] he would spend his time playing games in solitude. Because of his disdain for a coercive teaching style, Albert was often unpopular with teachers. His Greek teacher was so unimpressed with Albert's scholarship,[12] that he said Albert would fail at any occupation he undertook.

Despite the unfavorable reports, there was[13] also clues to Albert's potential: his musical interest and ability, his self-taught mastery of geometry and calculus, and his intense interest in how the world worked. Given a compass, young Albert found that the needle always pointed in the same direction. He was impressed by the mysterious behavior of such devices,[14]

and set out to learn more. He felt that behind worldly objects there was something "deeply hidden:[15]" the inner miracles that make up the outer world.

For good or bad, Albert Einstein's early years'[16] have contributed to a mystique that has never wore[17] off. Who knows in what child the next genius lurks?

1. *equation E = mc²*—Punctuation: comma unnecessary with essential appositive **[5.41 i]**
2. $E = mc^2$—Content: see illustration **[2.1]**
3. *mass* is simply *energy*—Content: see caption **[2.1]**
4. *frozen.*"—Punctuation: period inside quotation marks **[5.54]**
5. *his or her*—Usage: agreement of possessive pronoun with indefinite pronoun **[4.9]**
6. *Albert* the child—Punctuation: comma unnecessary with essential appositive **[5.41 i]**
   (Acceptable: *Albert the child, who*)
7. *people):*—Punctuation: colon outside parentheses **[5.14]**
8. *two)!*—Punctuation: exclamation point outside parentheses **[5.46]**
9. *children's*—Punctuation: *'s* used with possessive of plural not ending in *s* **[5.6]**
10. *strenuous* physical—Punctuation: comma unnecessary with noncoordinate modifier **[5.41 c]**
11. *Instead,*—Punctuation: comma used after introductory word **[5.25]**
12. *scholarship* that—Punctuation: comma unnecessary when dependent clause follows main clause **[5.41 l]**
13. there *were* also clues—Usage: agreement of verb with subject (when verb is placed before subject) **[4.3]**
14. *devices* and—Punctuation: comma unnecessary with compound predicate **[5.41 h]**
15. "*deeply hidden*":—Punctuation: colon outside quotation marks **[5.14]**

16. *years*—Punctuation: apostrophe unnecessary [5.3]
17. has never *worn*—Grammar: past participle with present perfect tense [3.29, 3.36]

E for Einstein Corrected

Many of us know Albert Einstein for his equation $E = mc^2$ and the idea that mass is simply energy that is "frozen." Each of us who has heard of Albert Einstein and his theories has his or her image of Albert the genius. However, what do we know of Albert the child who became the famous man?

Albert was seen as an unpromising youth for several reasons (in fact, his success would surprise many people): his early slowness in learning, his disdain for physical activity, and his dislike of school. Albert did not learn to speak until he was three years old (not by the usual age two)! He did not enjoy outdoor children's games; he complained that strenuous physical activity made him dizzy. Instead, he would spend his time playing games in solitude. Because of his disdain for a coercive teaching style, Albert was often unpopular with teachers. His Greek teacher was so unimpressed with Albert's scholarship that he said Albert would fail at any occupation he undertook.

Despite the unfavorable reports, there were also clues to Albert's potential: his musical interest and ability, his self-taught mastery of geometry and calculus, and his intense interest in how the world worked. Given a compass, young Albert found that the needle always pointed in the same direction. He was impressed by the mysterious behavior of such devices and set out to learn more. He felt that behind worldly objects there was something "deeply hidden": the inner miracles that make up the outer world.

For good or bad, Albert Einstein's early years have contributed to a mystique that has never worn off. Who knows in what child the next genius lurks?

21. Club Dread

17 errors—3 content; 2 grammar; 7 punctuation; 3 spelling; 2 usage

Club Dread Errors

Do you have a

notion for motion, a
need for speed, or a
yearn for the burn?

If you answered "Yes"![1] and have passed a rigerous[2] physical exam, come test your metal[3]. (Warning: this resort is for the intrepid-action[4] addict[5] not for the faint of heart!)

We offer a wide variety of action-packed sports, including zesty winter challenges (cool)![6] and sizzling summer adventures (hot!). See details on page 4. (Note that waterskiing and snow skiing is[7] offered [8]seasonally only[8].)

Read what [9]customers, Do, Chang, and Folly,[9] have to say about are[10] resort:

"The club fits my needs 'to a tee.[11]"
"It gives Bob and I[12] the biggest thrill!"
"This is definitely not for 'wimps'."[13]

By the time you leave, you will have confronted your fears, rose[14] to their challenge, and conquered those fears!

Please give all information indicated.

Name: *Jo Muletti*

Phone: *(206) 555-0029*

Age: *18*[15]

E-mail Address: *jmulet@abc.net*

Emergency contact:

Martha Turner, (206) 555-8893

Do you meet physical criterions[16]**?** [17]

Will you sign a release form? Yes

1. *"Yes!"*—Punctuation: exclamation point inside quotation marks **[5.44]**
2. *rigorous*—Spelling **[6.7]**
3. *mettle*—Spelling **[6.1]**
4. *intrepid action*—Punctuation: hyphen unnecessary with noncoordinate modifier **[3.11]**
5. *addict,* not—Punctuation: comma used with contrasting expressions **[5.34]**
6. *(cool!)*—Punctuation: exclamation point inside parenthesis **[5.46]**
7. *are*—Usage: agreement of verb with compound subjects joined by *and* **[4.6]**
8. *year-round*—Content: see caption **[2.1]**
9. *customers Do, Chang, and Folly*—Punctuation: comma unnecessary with essential appositive **[5.41 i]**
10. *our*—Usage: word pair (our/are) **[4.18]**
11. *tee."'*—Punctuation: quotation marks denote special word usage (single quotation marks for special words inside quote) **[5.64, 5.67]**
12. Bob and *me*—Grammar: pronoun used as object **[3.22]**
13. *wimps."'*—Punctuation: period inside quotation marks (both sets) **[5.54]**
14. *risen*—Grammar: past participle (used in future perfect tense) **[3.29, 3.36]**
15. *17*—Content: see caption **[2.1]**
16. *criteria*—Spelling **[6.5]**
17. **criteria?** *Yes*—Content: see caption **[2.1]**

Club Dread Corrected

Do you have a

> ### notion for motion, a
> ### need for speed, or a
> ### yearn for the burn?

If you answered "Yes!" and have passed a rigorous physical exam, come test your mettle. (Warning: this resort is

for the intrepid action addict, not for the faint of heart!)

We offer a wide variety of action-packed sports, including zesty winter challenges (cool!) and sizzling summer adventures (hot!). See details on page 4. (Note that waterskiing and snow skiing are offered year-round.)

Read what customers Do, Chang, and Folly have to say about our resort

> "The club fits my needs 'to a tee.'"
> "It gives Bob and me the biggest thrill!"
> "This is definitely not for 'wimps.'"

By the time you leave, you will have confronted your fears, risen to their challenge, and conquered those fears!

Please give all information indicated.

Name: Jo Muletti

Phone: (206) 555-0029

Age: 17

Email Address: jmulet@abc.net

Emergency contact:

Martha Turner, (206) 555-8893

Do you meet physical criteria? Yes

Will you sign a release form? Yes

22. To Sea by the Stars

15 errors—2 content; 1 capitalization; 2 grammar; 7 punctuation; 3 usage

To Sea by the Stars Errors

For centuries, sailors have measured their ships' positions at sea by observing the Sun, Moon[1] planets, and stars. Measuring latitude was relatively easy since it was based on the altitude of the Sun above the horizon. However, it wasn't until the 18th century that sailors were able to devise a method for determining longitude. Called "celestial navigation",[2] this[3] is based on the idea that a heavenly body is directly over a specific point on the earth's surface at a giving[4] time. By observing the direction of a star from the ship and measuring its angle above the horizon, the navigator can ascertain how far the ship is from the earthly position of the star. Earthly position indicates where a heavenly body would be,[5] if it were to drop [6]at an angle[6] to the earth.

To find the exact position of the ship, the navigator picks three stars. Using a sextant (an instrument developed in the mid-1800s[7]), the navigator measures the angle that each make[8] with the horizon. The angle of each star and the time it was measured is[9] recorded.

The navigator then consults an Almanac[10], which lists the predicted,[11] earthly positions of selective[12] heavenly bodies based on their angles at specific times and dates, and plots these positions on a map of the area. The earthly position is the center of an imaginary circle called a "circle of position." Because the circles are so large, the navigator usually draws only a portion of each[13] indicating where the circles overlap (as shown in the illustration.)[14] This intersection of the three lines forms a triangle,[15] the ship's position is at the approximate center of this triangle.

1. *Moon,* planets—Punctuation: comma used after words in a series **[5.22]**
2. *navigation,"*—Punctuation: comma used inside quotation marks **[5.40]**
3. *this method*—Grammar: ambiguous pronoun reference **[3.19]**
4. *given*—Grammar: verbal (participle used as adjective) **[3.37]**
5. *be if*—Punctuation: comma unnecessary when dependent clause follows main clause **[5.41 l]**
6. *straight*—Content: see illustration **[2.1]**
   (Acceptable: *at a 90° angle*)
7. *mid-1700s*—Content: see caption

(18th century would be 1700s) **[2.1]** (Acceptable: *mid-18th century*)

8. *makes*—Usage: agreement of verb with indefinite pronoun **[4.8]**
9. *are* recorded—Usage: agreement of verb with compound subjects joined by *and* **[4.6]**
10. *almanac*—Capital: unnecessary (not used as proper noun) **[1.4]**
11. *predicted earthly* —Punctuation: comma unnecessary with noncoordinate adjectives **[5.41 c]**
12. *selected*—Usage: word pair (selected/selective) **[4.18]**
13. *each*, indicating—Punctuation: comma used with nonessential participial phrase **[5.31]**
14. *illustration).*—Punctuation: period outside parenthesis **[5.55]**
15. *triangle;* the—Punctuation: semicolon separates main clauses joined without coordinating conjunction **[5.68]**

To Sea by the Stars Corrected

For centuries, sailors have measured their ships' positions at sea by observing the Sun, Moon, planets, and stars. Measuring latitude was relatively easy since it was based on the altitude of the Sun above the horizon. However, it wasn't until the 18th century that sailors were able to devise a method for determining longitude. Called "celestial navigation," this method is based on the idea that a heavenly body is directly over a specific point on the earth's surface at a given time. By observing the direction of a star from the ship and measuring its angle above the horizon, the navigator can ascertain how far the ship is from the earthly position of the star. Earthly position indicates where a heavenly body would be if it were to drop directly to the earth.

To find the exact position of the ship, the navigator picks three stars. Using a sextant (an instrument developed in the mid-1700s), the navigator measures the angle that each makes with the horizon. The angle of each star and the time it was measured are recorded.

The navigator then consults an almanac, which lists the predicted earthly positions of selected heavenly bodies based on their angles at specific times and dates, and plots these positions on a map of the area. The earthly position is the center of an imaginary circle called a "circle of position." Because the circles are so large, the navigator usually draws only a portion of each, indicating where the circles overlap (as shown in the illustration). This intersection of the three lines forms a triangle; the ship's position is at the approximate center of this triangle.

23. Campus Life

18 errors—1 content; 3 capitalization; 3 grammar; 8 punctuation; 3 usage

Campus Life Errors

> 852 College Blvd.
> Dormitory A-4
> Los Angeles, CA 90001
> September 1, 1999

Dear Rochelle[1]

I have finally arrived at the University of California. It is much different from life in the [2]south and Junior[3] college! Luckily, I got a campus tour before classes started.

Right now, I'm in the middle of tryouts for the women's dance team. The team all works[4] very hard together to get the best new members. I hope my cheerleading experience and eleven years of dancing gives[5] me an edge on the competition. At this point, though, it's anyone's guess as to who will make the team.

I'd also like to sign up for the business club here on campus, although I might have missed the [6]new member[6] deadline. A few of the people who live in my dormitory is[7] part of the club and say it's one of the most prestigious business clubs

around. If I [8]would have known[8] about it sooner, I'd have made it to the first meeting. (Who would have thought sign-ups were the week before classes?)

My roommate and me[9] are getting along well. If we were a little less busy, we'd have more time to just [10]hang out."[10] She's taking 19 units! (Last semester, she made straight As[11] with 17 units)![12] Can you imagine anyone taking such a heavy load.[13] I wonder how she does it?[14]

I must go now, Rochelle. The dance team meets in [15]15 minutes[15]! I'm sure by the time I have a chance to write to you again, the Fall[16] semester already will have flew[17] by. Take care of yourself, and write back soon.

> Love[18]
> *Natalie*

1. *Rochelle,*—Punctuation: comma used after greeting of a friendly letter **[5.19]**
2. *South*—Capital: direction used as proper geographic name **[1.6]**
3. *junior*—Capital: unnecessary (not used as a proper adjective) **[1.5]**
4. *work*—Usage: agreement of verb with collective subject used in a plural sense **[4.4]**
5. *give*—Usage: agreement of verb with compound subjects joined by *and* **[4.6]**
6. *new-member* deadline—Punctuation: hyphen used in compound adjective **[5.48]**
7. *are*—Usage: agreement of verb with indefinite pronoun (few/are) **[4.8]**
8. I *had known*—Grammar: avoid *would have* in *if* clause (use past perfect tense) **[3.31]**
9. *I*—Grammar: pronoun used as subject **[3.22]**
10. *"hang out."*—Punctuation: quotation marks denote special word usage **[5.64]**
11. *A's*—Punctuation: apostrophe used with plural of letter **[5.2]**

12. *units!)* — Punctuation: exclamation point inside parenthesis **[5.46]**

13. *load?* — Punctuation: question mark after direct question **[5.56]**

14. *it.* — Punctuation: question mark unnecessary after indirect question **[5.57]**

15. *30 minutes* — Content: see caption and illustration **[2.1]**

16. *fall* — Capital: unnecessary in season (unless personified) **[1.12]**

17. *flown* — Grammar: past participle (used in future perfect tense) **[3.29, 3.36]**

18. *Love,* — Punctuation: comma after closing of letter **[5.21]**

Campus Life Corrected

852 College Blvd.
Dormitory A-4
Los Angeles, CA 90001
September 1, 1999

Dear Rochelle,

I have finally arrived at the University of California. It is much different from life in the South and junior college! Luckily, I got a campus tour before classes started.

Right now, I'm in the middle of tryouts for the women's dance team. The team all work very hard together to get the best new members. I hope my cheerleading experience and eleven years of dancing give me an edge on the competition. At this point, though, it's anyone's guess as to who will make the team.

I'd also like to sign up for the business club here on campus, although I might have missed the new-member deadline. A few of the people who live in my dormitory are part of the club and say it's one of the most prestigious business clubs around. If I had known about it sooner, I'd have made it to the first meeting. (Who would have thought sign-ups were the week before classes?)

My roommate and I are getting along well. If we were a little less busy, we'd have more time to just "hang out." She's

taking 19 units! (Last semester, she made straight A's with 17 units!) Can you imagine anyone taking such a heavy load? I wonder how she does it.

I must go now, Rochelle. The dance team meets in 30 minutes! I'm sure by the time I have a chance to write to you again, the fall semester already will have flown by. Take care of yourself, and write back soon.

Love,
Natalie

24. Gearing Up for Fun

16 errors—1 content; 1 grammar; 8 punctuation; 2 spelling; 4 usage

Gearing Up for Fun Errors

**Directions for Playing "In Gear"
(2–4 players)**

Object:

Move all six of your peg[1] from Start to Finish. This must be done by turning a gears[2] so that pegs from one gear lined[3] up with a hole in the next gear.

Method—[4]

1. Place a peg in the Start hole at the beginning of a turn. (The Start hole is the one to which the stationery[5] arrow points.)

2. Shake,[6] and throw the dice to get the number of moves allowed for the turn. Pegs are moved by turning the gears in which they ride. (Remember this: when you move one gear, both gears move!) One move equals 1/12 revolution of the gear. (Each hole moves to the position of an adjacent hole).[7]

3. Turn both gears by pushing the first gear at Start (you may push it either clockwise or counterclockwise) to get your peg as close as possible to the second gear. You may not accede[8] the number of allowed moves. An example follows:

If you threw an "8",[9] you could get your Start peg to line up with the second gear by turning the first gear clockwise[10] by four teeth. After transferring a peg[11] you would still have four moves left (eight minus four;[12]) therefore, you could turn the gear until your peg was one tooth from Finish[13]

4. Continue to play[14] following the rules[14] until all your pegs have reach[15] Finish. The first player too[16] reach this goal wins!

1. *pegs*—Usage: agreement of indefinite pronoun with antecedent noun (all/pegs) **[4.5]**
2. a *gear*—Usage: agreement of adjective (article) with noun (a/gear) **[4.10]** (Acceptable: turning *gears* or turning *the gears*)
3. *line*—Usage: agreement of verb with subject (pegs/line) **[4.3]** (Acceptable: *are lined*)
4. *Method:*—Punctuation: colon introduces a list of items **[5.10]**
5. *stationary*—Spelling **[6.1]**
6. *Shake* and—Punctuation: comma unnecessary in compound predicate **[5.41 h]**
7. *hole.)*—Punctuation: period inside parenthesis **[5.55]**
8. *exceed*—Usage: word pair (exceed/accede) **[4.18]**
9. *"8,"*—Punctuation: comma used inside quotation marks **[5.40]**
10. *counterclockwise*—Content: see illustration **[2.1]**
11. *peg,*—Punctuation: comma used after introductory phrase **[5.26]**
12. *four);*—Punctuation: semicolon outside parenthesis **[5.71]**
13. *Finish.*—Punctuation: period used after a declarative sentence **[5.52]**
14. *play, following the rules,*—Punctuation: commas used with nonessential adverb phrase **[5.31]**

(Acceptable: *play, following the rules until…*)
15. have *reached*—Grammar: past participle (used in present perfect tense) **[3.29, 3.36]**
16. *to*—Spelling **[6.1]**

Gearing Up for Fun Corrected
Directions for Playing "In Gear"
(2–4 players)

Object:

Move all six of your pegs from Start to Finish. This must be done by turning a gear so that pegs from one gear line up with a hole in the next gear.

Method:

1. Place a peg in the Start hole at the beginning of a turn. (The Start hole is the one to which the stationary arrow points.)

2. Shake and throw the dice to get the number of moves allowed for the turn. Pegs are moved by turning the gears in which they ride. (Remember this: when you move one gear, both gears move!) One move equals 1/12 revolution of the gear. (Each hole moves to the position of an adjacent hole.)

3. Turn both gears by pushing the first gear at Start (you may push it either clockwise or counterclockwise) to get your peg as close as possible to the second gear. You may not exceed the number of allowed moves. An example follows:

If you threw an "8," you could get your Start peg to line up with the second gear by turning the first gear counterclockwise by four teeth. After transferring a peg, you would still have four moves left (eight minus four); therefore, you could turn the gear until your peg was one tooth from Finish.

4. Continue to play, following the rules, until all your pegs have reached Finish. The first player to reach this goal wins!

25. The Gypsy Life

15 errors—3 content; 1 capitalization; 3 grammar; 2 punctuation; 6 usage

The Gypsy Life Errors

Gypsies have long been a subject of interest to many people. Their nomadic lifestyle and professions [1]fortune telling and animal tamer,[2] for example) have created an image of the exotic Gypsy.

The nomadic Gypsies travel seasonal[3] along specific routes that connect him[4] to other bands of Gypsies. Their migratory nature has taken them from their origins in India to [5]northern Europe[5] in the eleventh century, to southwestern[6] Europe in the fourteenth century, and to western Europe in the fifteenth century[7] and the second half of the twentieth century has seen Gypsies spread throughout north[8] and South America and Asia[9]. Estimating their population has been almost impossible because of their extensive and constant travel. At present, there may be as little[10] as one million or as many as six million.

Traditionally, Gypsies have pursued occupations that make it easy to travel. Men were metalsmiths, musicians, livestock traders, and animal trainers and exhibitors. Women were [11]most common[11] fortune tellers, beggars, entertainers, and potion sellers.

Today, industrialism and growing urban influences are changing the traditional Gypsy ways. [12]Instead of doing metal work, mechanics is now a common occupation for Gypsies.[12] Their modes of transportation has[13] shifted from riding horses and walking to driving cars and flying. Now, there are reports that even traveling is declining. How the future

[14]effect[15] Gypsy culture remains to be seen. Is the Gypsy culture on the brink of extinction or simply in the process of evolution?

1. *(fortune...*example)—Punctuation: parentheses used (in pairs) to enclose supplementary words **[5.49]**
2. animal *taming*—Usage: gerund (parallel structure) **[4.14]**
3. *seasonally*—Grammar: adverb modifies verb **[3.4]**
4. *them*—Usage: agreement of pronoun with noun **[4.2]**
5. *the Middle East*—Content: see caption and illustration **[2.1]**
6. *southeastern*—Content: See caption and illustration **[2.1]**
7. *century. The second*—Punctuation: run-on sentence **[5.81]**
8. *North*—Capital: proper noun **[1.4]**
9. *Australia*—Content: see caption and illustration **[2.1]**
10. as *few* as—Usage: word pair (less or little/fewer) **[4.18]**
11. *most commonly*—Grammar: superlative adverb **[3.6]**
12. *Instead of metal work, mechanics*—Usage: dangling modifier **[4.16]** (Acceptable: *Instead of doing metal work, Gypsies are now working as mechanics.*, etc.)
13. *have*—Usage: agreement of verb with subject (modes/have) **[4.3]**
14. *will* affect—Grammar: helping verb used in future tense **[3.29, 3.33]**
15. *affect*—Usage: word pair (affect/effect) **[4.18]**

The Gypsy Life Corrected

Gypsies have long been a subject of interest to many people. Their nomadic lifestyle and professions (fortune telling and animal taming, for example) have created an image of the exotic Gypsy.

The nomadic Gypsies travel seasonally along specific routes that connect them to other bands of Gypsies. Their migratory nature has taken them from their origins in India to the Middle East in the eleventh century, to southeastern Europe in the fourteenth century, and to western Europe in the fifteenth century. The second half of the twentieth century has seen Gypsies spread throughout North and South America and Australia. Estimating their population has been almost impossible because of their extensive and constant travel. At present, there may be as few as one million or as many as six million.

Traditionally, Gypsies have pursued occupations that make it easy to travel. Men were metalsmiths, musicians, livestock traders, and animal trainers and exhibitors. Women were most commonly fortune tellers, beggars, entertainers, and potion sellers.

Today, industrialism and growing urban influences are changing the traditional Gypsy ways. Instead of metal work, mechanics is now a common occupation for Gypsies. Their modes of transportation have shifted from riding horses and walking to driving cars and flying. Now, there are reports that even traveling is declining. How the future will affect Gypsy culture remains to be seen. Is the Gypsy culture on the brink of extinction or simply in the process of evolution?

26. Waltzing into Trouble

18 errors—1 content; 1 capitalization; 4 grammar; 7 punctuation; 2 spelling; 3 usage

Waltzing into Trouble Errors

I had [1]scarcely never been[1] so embarrassed in my life as I was at the mayor's ball!

My [2]friend, Greg,[2] and I had been taking lessons in ballroom dance for several months, and we just had to show off our new skills to the revered attendees. The viennese[3] waltz can be difficult to execute, but we thought we would navigate the floor with no problem.

All started well. With the downbeat, we commenced our ill[4] fated swirling tour, weaving between and around other dancers. (We even turned up our noses at other dancer's[5] steps.) My steps were well placed when I crossed my feet for the turns,[6] my dance form was implacable[7].

A couple moving into our path caused a real turn of events. To avoid them, Greg turned us in a new direction. [8]Momentarily distracted, my next step was faulty, one heel catching in my other shoe.[8] The floor seemed to fly up at us before I knew what has[9] happened! Some of the other dancers barely avoided spilling on top of us, while others struggled to suppressing[10] there[11] laughter. I just wished the floor would open up and swallow ourselves[12].

Despite the fiasco, we remembered Instructor Kims[13] motto that "the show must go on",[14] and we got up. We dusted us[15] off,[16] and pretended that we couldn't careless[17] about falling. We put the best face on a bad situation by finishing in style[18] without showing any embarrassment.[18]

1. ~~scarcely~~ never been—Usage: double negative **[4.19]**
   (Acceptable: scarcely *ever* been; scarcely ~~never~~ been)
2. *friend Greg*—Punctuation: commas unnecessary with essential appositive **[5.41 i]**
3. *Viennese*—Capital: proper adjective **[1.5]**
4. *ill-fated*—Punctuation: hyphen used in compound adjective **[5.48]**
5. *dancers'*—Punctuation: apostrophe used with possessive of plural ending in *s* **[5.5]**
6. *turns;*—Punctuation: semicolon separates main clauses joined without coordinating conjunction (corrects comma splice) **[5.68]**
7. *impeccable*—Usage: word pair (impeccable/implacable **[4.18]**
8. *Because I was momentarily...*—Usage: dangling modifier **[4.16]**

(Acceptable: *Momentarily distracted, I caught the heel of one shoe in the other shoe.*)

9. *had* happened—Grammar: helping verb (used in past perfect) **[3.29, 3.33]**
10. to *suppress*—Grammar: infinitive **[3.39]**
11. *their*—Spelling **[6.1]**
12. *us*—Grammar: pronoun used as object (not reflexive pronoun) **[3.22]**
13. *Kim's*—Punctuation: *'s* used with singular possessive **[5.4]**
14. *on,"*—Punctuation: comma used inside quotation marks **[5.40]**
15. *ourselves*—Grammar: reflexive pronoun **[3.25]**
16. *off and*—Punctuation: comma unnecessary in compound predicate **[5.41 h]**
17. *care less*—Spelling **[6.6]**
    Note: for information on the phrase "couldn't care less," see Content **[2.1]**
18. style, *though we were still embarrassed.*—Content: see caption (their faces remained red) **[2.1]**
    (Acceptable: *in style., in style but with embarrassment.; style without mishap.,* etc.)

Waltzing into Trouble Corrected

I had scarcely been so embarrassed in my life as I was at the mayor's ball!

My friend Greg and I had been taking lessons in ballroom dance for several months, and we just had to show off our new skills to the revered attendees. The Viennese waltz can be difficult to execute, but we thought we would navigate the floor with no problem.

All started well. With the downbeat, we commenced our ill-fated swirling tour, weaving between and around other dancers. (We even turned up our noses at other dancers' steps.) My steps were well placed when I crossed my feet for the turns; my dance form was impeccable.

A couple moving into our path caused a real turn of events. To avoid them, Greg turned us in a new direction. Because I

was momentarily distracted, my next step was faulty, one heel catching in my other shoe. The floor seemed to fly up at us before I knew what had happened! Some of the other dancers barely avoided spilling on top of us, while others struggled to suppress their laughter. I just wished the floor would open up and swallow us.

Despite the fiasco, we remembered Instructor Kim's motto that "the show must go on," and we got up. We dusted ourselves off and pretended that we couldn't care less about falling. We put the best face on a bad situation by finishing in style, though we were still embarrassed.

27. Supply and Demand

16 errors—2 content; 1 capitalization; 6 punctuation; 3 spelling; 4 usage

Supply and Demand Errors

Two of the most basic concepts of economics are supply and demand. Supply is how much is available, and demand is how much [1]people are wanting[1]. These concepts can be applied to almost any good or service.

For example, the supply of bread will raise[2] if it's in demand because sellers know that people will buy them[3]. However, the supply of bread will fall if people no longer want to buy it (a decrease in it's[4] demand) because sellers won't maintain a supply of something they can't sell.

[5]Often shown as curves on graphs, economists make a habit of tracking supply and demand.[5] Supply increases as demand decreases,[6] the opposite is also true. On a graph, these curves would meet at some point. This intersection is called:[7] the equilibrium level because it is the level of highest satisfaction for both buyer and seller. Excluding other factors[8] the equilibrium level will result in supply matching demand.

One thing often tracked on a supply-demand [9]Graph is price. For example, supply can be shown as the number of loaves of bread offered on grocery store shelves each week, and demand can be shown as the price paid for each loaf of bread. According to the graph (which shows that 15[10] loafs[11] would be bought at a price of $2.25)[12] the equilibrium price for 30 loaves of bread is $1.25[13] each.

In the real world[14] though[14] the graph is just a model. Experience drives today's economic markets more than any economist[15] manufactured model. Still, supply and demand are powerful phenomenon[16] that every buyer and seller should consider.

1. *is wanted*—Usage: parallel structure **[4.12]**
   (Acceptable: *people want*)
2. *rise*—Usage: word pair (rise/raise) **[4.18]**
3. *it*—Usage: agreement of pronoun with noun **[4.2]**
4. *its*—Spelling (or Punctuation: unnecessary apostrophe) **[6.1]**
5. *Economists make a habit of tracking supply and demand, which are often shown as curves on graphs.*—Usage: dangling modifier **[4.16]**
6. *decreases;*—Punctuation: semicolon separates main clauses joined without coordinating conjunction (corrects comma splice) **[5.68]**
7. *called the*—Punctuation: colon unnecessary **[5.13]**
8. *factors, the*—Punctuation: comma used after introductory phrase **[5.26]**
9. *graph*—Capital: unnecessary (not used as proper noun) **[1.4]**
10. *10*—Content: see illustration **[2.1]**
    (Acceptable: leave *15* and change $ amount to *$1.75*)
11. *loaves*—Spelling **[6.3]**
12. *$2.25),*—Punctuation: comma used after introductory dependent clause) **[5.26]**
13. *$1*—Content: see illustration **[2.1]**
14. *world, though,*—Punctuation: comma used with sentence interrupter **[5.28]**

15. *economist-manufactured*—Punctuation: hyphen used in compound adjective **[5.48]**
    (Acceptable: *economist's manufactured*)
16. *phenomena*—Spelling **[6.5]**

Supply and Demand Corrected

Two of the most basic concepts of economics are supply and demand. Supply is how much is available; demand is how much is wanted. These concepts can be applied to almost any good or service.

For example, the supply of bread will rise if it's in demand because sellers know that people will buy it. However, the supply of bread will fall if people no longer want to buy it (a decrease in its demand) because sellers won't maintain a supply of something they can't sell.

Economists make a habit of tracking supply and demand, often shown as curves on graphs. Supply increases as demand decreases; the opposite is also true. On a graph, these curves would meet at some point. This intersection is called the equilibrium level because it is the level of highest satisfaction for both buyer and producer. Excluding other factors, the equilibrium level will result in supply matching demand.

One thing often tracked on a supply-demand graph is price. For example, supply can be shown as the number of loaves of bread offered on grocery store shelves each week, and demand can be shown as the price paid for each loaf of bread. According to the graph (which shows that 10 loaves would be bought at a price of $2.25), the equilibrium price for 30 loaves of bread is $1 each.

In the real world, though, the graph is just a model. Experience drives today's economic markets more than any economist-manufactured model. Still, supply and demand are powerful phenomenon that every buyer and seller should consider.

28. An Alternative American Story

18 errors—2 content; 2 capitalization; 2 grammar; 7 punctuation; 2 spelling; 3 usage

An Alternative American Story Errors

"What do you think of my idea"?[1] Ruth asked.

"I think your[2] better off in a creative writing class," Sula said with a chuckle. "Don't you dare write any of that on your history exam. You'll get laughed out of class. You know George Washington died in 1776 trying to cross the Delaware. He wasn't our first president,[3] everybody knows Abraham Lincoln he[4] was. Anyway, what's with that silly song you keep singing, "[5]stars and stripes forever[5]?"[6] You know our flag has only [7]two giant stars[7]."

"Sula, Lincoln wouldn't have been president at all if General Grant [8]would not have[8] disappeared three weeks before the 1866 election, but that's not the point. What if George Washington *had* crossed the Delaware? What if *we* had won the Colonial War? I wonder how different things would have been?[9] We might have been our own country in 1776, [10]ninety-eight[10] years before the Continental War of Independence. What if we had no East and West? What if we were living in a state right now, instead of in a territory?"

"Ruth," Sula said in exasperation, "Go[11] no farther[12]. Get[13] through to you is impossible! I'm going elsewhere too[14] study. I'll see you later. Good luck on your test. You'll need it." Sula left[15] her patience at an end.

[16]In her favorite notebook, Ruth sat down and began to write her story[16]. [17]Patriot's Tale[17] began as follows: "It all started on a cold night in December. The Delaware River was cold but not frozen[18] and visibility was good. Hoping for the best, General Washington ordered the surprise attack to commence..."

1. *idea?"*—Punctuation: question mark inside quotation marks when it applies to quoted material **[5.58]**
2. *you're*—Spelling **[6.1]**
3. *president;*—Punctuation: semicolon separates main clauses joined without coordinating conjunction (corrects comma splice) **[5.68, 5.81]**
4. *Lincoln* ~~he~~ *was*—Usage: unnecessary word **[4.19]**
5. *Stars and Stripes Forever*—Capital: title of song **[1.14]**
6. *Forever'?*—Punctuation: question mark outside quotation marks when it doesn't apply to quoted material **[5.59]**
7. *one giant star*—Content: see illustration **[2.1]** (Acceptable: *one giant star and thirteen stripes*)
8. Grant *hadn't* disappeared—Grammar: avoid *would have* in *if* clause (use past perfect tense) **[3.31]** (Acceptable: *had not*)
9. *been.*—Punctuation: question mark unnecessary after indirect question **[5.57]**
10. *ninety*—Content: see illustration **[2.1]**
11. *go*—Capital: unnecessary (divided quotation) **[1.2]**
12. *further*—Usage: word pair (further/farther) **[4.18]**
13. *Getting*—Grammar: verbal (gerund) **[3.38]**
14. *to*—Spelling **[6.1]**
15. *left,* her patience at an end—Punctuation: comma used with absolute phrase **[5.32]**
16. *Ruth sat down and began to write her story in her favorite notebook:*—Usage: dangling modifier **[4.16]** (Acceptable: *down and in her favorite notebook began... etc.*)
17. *"Patriot's Tale"*—Punctuation: quotation marks enclose story title **[5.63]**
18. *frozen,*—Punctuation: comma used before coordinating conjunction joining independent clauses **[5.37]**

An Alternative American Story Corrected

"What do you think of my idea?" Ruth asked.

"I think you're better off in a creative writing class," Sula said with a chuckle. "Don't you dare write any of that on your history exam. You'll get laughed out of class. You know George Washington died in 1776 trying to cross the Delaware. He wasn't our first president; everybody knows Abraham Lincoln was. Anyway, what's with that silly song you keep singing, 'Stars and Stripes Forever'? You know our flag has only one giant star."

"Sula, Lincoln wouldn't have been president at all if General Grant hadn't disappeared three weeks before the 1866 election, but that's not the point. What if George Washington *had* crossed the Delaware? What if *we* had won the Colonial War? I wonder how different things would have been. We might have been our own country in 1776, ninety years before the Continental War of Independence. What if we had no East and West? What if we were living in a state right now, instead of in a territory?"

"Ruth," Sula said in exasperation, "go no further. Getting through to you is impossible! I'm going elsewhere to study. I'll see you later. Good luck on your test. You'll need it." Sula left, her patience at an end.

Ruth sat down and began to write her story in her favorite notebook. "Patriot's Tale" began as follows: "It all started on a cold night in December. The Delaware River was cold but not frozen, and visibility was good. Hoping for the best, General Washington ordered the surprise attack to commence..."

29. An A+ for C++

16 errors—1 content; 1 capitalization; 5 grammar; 3 punctuation; 6 usage

An A+ for C++ Errors

I've been giving my future career a lot of thought and [1]now decided that I could best put my technical skills to use by becoming an educator. [2]As a teacher, my students[2] should be able to expect lessons with immediate feedback for her[3] answers. The problem is is[4] that the increasing size of classes are[5] making such goals more difficulter[6] than ever. That's why I plan to program the lessons myself in the C++ language (as learned from professor[7] Duong). With a computer program, students could do lessons at their own pace; the computer would not only ask questions tireless[8] but also tell whether they[9] are correct.

I'm now creating a program (a part of which you can see in the illustration at right[10] for identifying state capitals. The program will contain the following;[11] a "loop," which keeps asking for the correct input until it is entered; "if/else" statements (one of which is shown in the diagram;)[12] and some "while" statements. When students pick choice two, Denver, as the capital of California, they won't have to wait for me to tell them, "[13]You're full of beans!"[13] That's what my program will display.

Programming is such fun that I am anxious[14] to take my study of C++ even farther[15]. I'm sure that it will greatly benefit both my students and I[16]!

1. *have* now decided—Grammar: helping verb with present perfect tense **[3.29, 3.33]**
   (Acceptable: *thought, and I have now...*)
2. *As a teacher, I think my students...*—Usage: dangling modifier **[4.16]**
   (Acceptable: *My students should...*, *As students, people should...* etc.)
3. *their*—Usage: agreement of possessive pronoun with noun (students/their) **[4.1]**
   (Acceptable: if the noun in error 2 is changed, the students should use a pronoun that agrees with it)
4. problem is ~~is~~ that—Usage: unnecessary word **[4.19]**
5. *is*—Usage: agreement of verb with subject (size/is) **[4.3]**

6. *more difficult*—Grammar: comparative adjective [3.6]

7. *Professor* Duong—Capital: title used as part of name [1.8]

8. *tirelessly*—Grammar: adverb modifies verb [3.4]

9. *the students*—Grammar: ambiguous pronoun reference [3.19] (Acceptable: *the answers*)

10. *right)*—Punctuation: parentheses used (in pairs) to enclose supplementary words [5.49]

11. *following*:—Punctuation: colon introduces words that explain or illustrate [5.12]

12. *diagram);*—Punctuation: semicolon outside parenthesis [5.71]

13. *Sorry. The capital is another city.*—Content: see diagram [2.1]

14. *eager*—Usage: word pair (eager/anxious) [4.18]

15. *further*—Usage: word pair (further/farther) [4.18]

16. students and *me*—Grammar: pronoun used as object [3.22]

An A+ for C++ Corrected

I've been giving my future career a lot of thought and have now decided that I could best put my technical skills to use by becoming an educator. As a teacher, I think my students should be able to expect lessons with immediate feedback for their answers. The problem is that the increasing size of classes is making such goals more difficult than ever. That's why I plan to program the lessons myself in the C++ language (as learned from Professor Duong). With a computer program, students could do lessons at their own pace; the computer would not only ask questions tirelessly but also tell whether the students are correct.

I'm now creating a program (a part of which you can see in the illustration at right) for identifying state capitals. The program will contain the following: a "loop," which keeps asking for the correct input until it is entered; "if/else" statements (one of which is shown in the diagram); and some "while" statements. When students pick choice two, Denver, as the capital of California, they won't have to wait for me to tell them, "Sorry. The capital is another city." That's what my program will display.

Programming is such fun that I am eager to take my study of C++ even further. I'm sure that it will greatly benefit both my students and me!

30. Biking Trail Debate

18 errors—1 content; 1 capitalization; 3 grammar; 12 punctuation; 1 usage

Biking Trail Debate Errors

Last night, the city council heard arguments for and against the proposed mountain bike trail and training program. (Trail design would mimic the Bikersville, Ark[1,2] trail built in 1994).[3] As expected, Dan Jones of DJ Trail Bikes came out in favor. "Mountain bike riders are numerous," he contended, [4]and they deserve a safe place to ride.[4]

Gabe Cordova thought the trail would be "useless for most of we[5] taxpayers." Also opposing the issue, Lucy McGovern voiced concerns of some safety-minded citizens. "We are against the trail because mountain biking promotes careless behavior," she said. "Don't you remember what happened in May of [6]98 at that impromptu,[7] mens'[8] contest"?[9]

Teen biker Gwen Schaffer then expressed her view. "That[10] was caused by some [11]local guy[11] yelling, [12]You're a liar and a cheat!"[12] to another spectator and then pushing him in front of a racer," she argued.

"She's right," said captain[13] Armelando of the police force, "and accept[14] for that fiasco, the only problems have been caused by lack of facilities. Besides[15] we can prevent careless biking by requiring that each user passes[16] the safety course."

Several other citizens followed in expressing their views on the proposal. In spite of cost and safety concerns, however, most attendees were proponents. In summary, the following pluses were cited[17]

1) safety through training
2) convenience of location
3) outlet for teenagers' energy

Views will continue to be heard during the next two week's[18] meetings. The council will vote on the issue in three weeks.

1. *Ark.*—Punctuation: period after abbreviation **[5.53]**
   (Acceptable: *Arkansas*)
2. *Ark.,*—Punctuation: comma after state in sentence **[5.16]**
   (Acceptable: *Arkansas,*)
3. *1994.)*—Punctuation: period inside parentheses **[5.55]**
4. *"and they deserve a safe place to ride."*—Punctuation: quotation marks enclose both parts of divided quotation **[5.60]**
5. *us* taxpayers—Grammar: pronoun used as object **[3.22]**
6. *'98*—Punctuation: apostrophe replaces numerals in year **[5.1]**
7. *impromptu*—Punctuation: comma unnecessary with noncoordinate modifier **[5.41 c]**
8. *men's*—Punctuation: *'s* used with possessive of plural not ending in *s* **[5.6]**
9. *contest?"*—Punctuation: question mark inside quotation marks when it applies to quoted material **[5.58]**
10. *The accident*—Grammar: ambiguous pronoun reference **[3.19]**
    (Acceptable: *That incident*, etc.)
11. *out-of-towner*—Content: see caption **[2.1]**
12. *'You're a liar and a cheat!'*—Punctuation: single quotation marks enclose quote within quote **[5.65]**
13. *Captain* Armelando—Capital: title used as part of name **[1.8]**

14. *except*—Usage: word pair (except/accept) **[4.18]**
15. *Besides,*—Punctuation: comma used after introductory word **[5.25]**
16. *pass*—Grammar: subjunctive mood used in contrary-to-fact statement **[3.32]**
17. *cited:*—Punctuation: colon introduces a list of items **[5.10]**
18. *weeks'*—Punctuation: apostrophe with possessive of plural ending in *s* **[5.5]**

Biking Trail Debate Corrected

Last night, the city council heard arguments for and against the proposed mountain bike trail and training program. (Trail design would mimic the Bikersville, Ark., trail built in 1994.) As expected, Dan Jones of DJ Trail Bikes came out in favor. "Mountain bike riders are numerous," he contended, "and they deserve a safe place to ride."

Gabe Cordova thought the trail would be "useless for most of us taxpayers." Also opposing the issue, Lucy McGovern voiced concerns of some safety-minded citizens. "We are against the trail because mountain biking promotes careless behavior," she said. "Don't you remember what happened in May of '98 at that impromptu men's contest?"

Teen biker Gwen Schaffer then expressed her view. "That accident was caused by some out-of-towner yelling, 'You're a liar and a cheat!' to another spectator and then pushing him in front of a racer," she argued.

"She's right," said Captain Armelando of the police force, "and except for that fiasco, the only problems have been caused by lack of facilities. Besides, we can prevent careless biking by requiring that each user pass the safety course."

Several other citizens followed in expressing their views on the proposal. In spite of cost and safety concerns, however, most attendees were proponents. In summary, the following pluses were cited:

1) safety through training
2) convenience of location
3) outlet for teenagers' energy

Views will continue to be heard during the next two weeks' meetings. The council will vote on the issue in three weeks.

31. A View to a Job

17 errors—1 content; 1 capitalization; 2 grammar; 8 punctuation; 1 spelling; 4 usage

A View to a Job Errors

January 12, 2006

Angelique Giroux[1] Managing Editor
Snapshot
Washington Square
White Plains[2] NY,[3] 10609

Dear Ms. Giroux,[4]

As a magazine editor, you want a photographer you can count on to provide top-quality photos and also meet deadlines. I can do both. My name is Kamilah Desai, and I am applying for the special assignment advertised in *Snapshot*.

As you can see from my enclosed resume[5] I have traveled the world in search of interesting photo opportunities. My most recent assignment was a freelance job for an advertising agency in Hong Kong. I shot scenes of the fish markets to illustrated[6] a series of magazine ads,[7] that stressed the importance of tradition in a technologically advanced world. [8]Doing a job as it has been done for hundreds of years, the photos showed people etched in almost surreal timelessness.[8] I won an Eastman award for this[9]. The whole advertising team were[10] proud.

My favorite assignment so far has been the four years I spent as the [11]Senior Photographer[11] for *Utah Illustrated*, published by the state travel association. The opportunities to capture nature on film is[12] still very abundant in Utah. I found that a creative approach to such well

photographed targets as Bryce Canyon and Trolley Square can yield photos of places that, at the same time, [13]not only seem[13] familiar but also new.

Please find enclosed these three things[14] a packet of sample photographs I have taken, my resume, and my business card. If you wish to contact me immediately, please send me an e-mail message at [15]kdesai@adn.com[15].

Thank you for your time and consideration. I hope to here[16] from you soon.

Sincerely[17]
Kamilah Desai
Kamilah Desai

1. *Giroux,*—Punctuation: comma separates name and title **[5.20]**
2. *Plains, NY*—Punctuation: comma separates elements of address **[5.15]**
3. *NY 10609*—Punctuation: comma unnecessary before ZIP code **[5.15]**
4. *Giroux:*—Punctuation: colon used after greeting of a business letter **[5.9]**
5. *resume,*—Punctuation: comma used after introductory phrase **[5.26]**
6. *illustrate*—Grammar: verbal (infinitive used as adverb) **[3.39]**
7. *ads* that—Punctuation: comma unnecessary with essential clause **[5.41 i]**
8. *The photos showed people, etched in almost surreal timelessness, doing a job as it has been done for hundreds of years.*—Usage: dangling modifier **[4.16]**
   (Acceptable: *The photos showed people etched…etc.,* also, any other grammatically correct sentence that is logical for the context)
9. *this series*—Grammar: ambiguous pronoun reference **[3.19]**
   (Acceptable: *assignment, spread, series of photos, etc.*)
10. *was*—Usage: agreement of verb with collective subject used in a singular sense **[4.4]**
11. *senior photographer*—Capital: unnec-

essary (title not used as part of name) **[1.8]**

12. *are*—Usage: agreement of verb with subject (opportunities/are) **[4.3]**

13. *seem not only*—Usage: correlative conjunctions (*not only...but also*) each followed by parallel phrase **[4.13]** (Acceptable: move *seem* immediately after *that*)

14. *things:*—Punctuation: colon introduces a list of items **[5.10]**

15. *kamdesai@adn.com*—Content: see illustration (business card) **[2.1]**

16. *hear*—Spelling **[6.1]**

17. *Sincerely,*—Punctuation: comma after closing of a letter **[5.21]**

A View to a Job Corrected

January 12, 2006

Angelique Giroux, Managing Editor
Snapshot
Washington Square
White Plains, NY 10609

Dear Ms. Giroux:

As a magazine editor, you want a photographer you can count on to provide top-quality photos and also meet deadlines. I can do both. My name is Kamilah Desai, and I am applying for the special assignment advertised in *Snapshot*.

As you can see from my enclosed resume, I have traveled the world in search of interesting photo opportunities. My most recent assignment was a freelance job for an advertising agency in Hong Kong. I shot scenes of the fish markets to illustrate a series of magazine ads that stressed the importance of tradition in a technologically advanced world. The photos showed people, etched in almost surreal timelessness, doing a job as it has been done for hundreds of years. I won an Eastman award for this series. The whole advertising team was proud.

My favorite assignment so far has been the four years I spent as the senior pho-

tographer for *Utah Illustrated*, published by the state travel association. The opportunities to capture nature on film are still very abundant in Utah. I found that a creative approach to such well photographed targets as Bryce Canyon and Trolley Square can yield photos that, at the same time, seem not only familiar but also new.

Please find enclosed these three things: a packet of sample photographs I have taken, my resume, and my business card. If you wish to contact me immediately, please send me an e-mail message at kamdesai@adn.com.

Thank you for your time and consideration. I hope to hear from you soon.

Sincerely,
Kamilah Desai
Kamilah Desai

32. Succeeding in Business

18 errors—1 content; 3 grammar; 8 punctuation; 6 usage

Succeeding in Business Errors

Many people think they could create a successful business, but few make the dream a reality. The formula for growing a business may seem simple ([1]you plan you work you succeed[1]), but don't be fooled. If success was[2] easy, most of us would be wealthy! Long and grueling are[3] the road to success, and you must often work like a dog—a dog who[4] is racing against the fastest of competitors!

Do you have what it takes to be a successful entrepreneur? Wanda[5] soul[6] proprietor of Wanda's Widgets, has found the following traits essential for her success in business.

Positive Attitude: Can you remain optimistic through hard times? It helps to be a confident[7] cheerful owner. A delay in profits have[8] frustrated many competitors,[9] however, Wanda has stuck it out. It is her[10] who now enjoys a flourishing trade.

Resources: Have you saved enough seed"[11] money to support the business for a few years? Many businesses take several years to become profitable. Wanda's Widgets, for example, was not profitable until the third[12] year. She had to be thrifty.

People Skills: Do you get along and communicate well with people? Many companies[13] failures can be traced to miscommunication and strife. Wanda was always clear and fair in dealing with [14]an employee, knowing that they were[14] one of the company's greatest assets.

Knowledge: Do you have enough knowledge about your product and how to market it? Wanda already had experience and knowledge,[15] what she didn't know[16] she learned in night classes.

Need to Achieve: Do you want success so badly that you would do anything necessary to get it? Only the strongest desire will keep you from quitting. Wanda thought of giving up; however, when her company announces their[17] annual profit, she's glad she has stuck with it!

Having review[18] the above requirements, you should have an idea of your own potential for business. Will yours be the next multimillion-dollar success?

1. *you plan, you work, you succeed* — Punctuation: comma used after independent clauses (short and parallel) **[5.23]**
   (Acceptable: *you plan, you work, and you succeed*)
2. *were* — Grammar: subjunctive mood used in contrary-to-fact statement **[3.32]**
3. *is* — Usage: agreement of verb with subject when verb is placed before the subject **[4.3]**
4. *that* — Usage: pronoun *that* refers to animals that are not personified **[4.2]**
5. *Wanda,* — Punctuation: comma used with nonessential appositive **[5.29]**
6. *sole* — Usage: word pair (soul/sole) **[4.18]**

7. *confident, cheerful* — Punctuation: comma separates coordinate adjectives **[5.24]**
   (Acceptable: *confidently cheerful*)
8. *has* — Usage: agreement of verb with subject (separated) (*delay/has*) **[4.3]**
9. *competitors;* — Punctuation: semicolon used before conjunctive adverb joining independent clauses **[5.69]**
10. *she* — Grammar: nominative case used with the verb *to be* **[3.23]**
11. *"seed"* — Punctuation: quotation marks denote special word usage **[5.64]**
12. *fifth* — Content: see illustration **[2.1]**
13. *companies'* — Punctuation: apostrophe used with possessive of plural ending in *s* **[5.5]**
14. an employee...*he or she was* — Usage: agreement of pronoun and verb with noun **[4.3, 4.2]**
    (Acceptable: an employee...*he was...*, an employee...*she was...*, also *employees*...they were)
15. *knowledge;* — Punctuation: semicolon separates main clauses joined without coordinating conjunctions (corrects comma splice) **[5.68]**
16. *know,* — Punctuation: comma used to avoid ambiguity **[5.36]**
17. *its* — Usage: agreement of possessive pronoun with collective subject used in singular sense **[4.5]**
18. having *reviewed* — Grammar: verbal (participle used as adjective) **[3.37]**

Succeeding in Business Corrected

Many people think they could create a successful business, but few make the dream a reality. The formula for growing a business may seem simple (you plan, you work, you succeed), but don't be fooled. If success were easy, most of us would be wealthy! Long and grueling is the road to success, and you must often work like a dog—a dog that is racing against the fastest of competitors!

Do you have what it takes to be a successful entrepreneur? Wanda, sole proprietor of Wanda's Widgets, has found the following traits essential for her success in business.

Positive Attitude: Can you remain optimistic through hard times? It helps to be a confident, cheerful owner. A delay in profits has frustrated many competitors; however, Wanda has stuck it out. It is she who now enjoys a flourishing trade.

Resources: Have you saved enough "seed" money to support the business for a few years? Many businesses take several years to become profitable. Wanda's Widgets, for example, was not profitable until the fifth year. She had to be thrifty.

People Skills: Do you get along and communicate well with people? Many companies' failures can be traced to miscommunication and strife. Wanda was always clear and fair in dealing with an employee, knowing that he or she was one of the company's greatest assets.

Knowledge: Do you have enough knowledge about your product and how to market it? Wanda already had experience and knowledge; what she didn't know, she learned in night classes.

Need to Achieve: Do you want success so badly that you would do anything necessary to get it? Only the strongest desire will keep you from quitting. Wanda thought of giving up; however, when her company announces its annual profit, she's glad she has stuck with it!

Having reviewed the above requirements, you should have an idea of your own potential for business. Will yours be the next multimillion-dollar success?

33. A Patent Lie?

18 errors—2 content; 3 grammar; 9 punctuation; 4 usage

A Patent Lie? Errors

Thaddeus related the following story at the June,[1] [2]99 Hoax Masters Club meeting:

"Driving home last week, [3]my eyes[3] met with an unusual sight: a huge saucer was spinning north[4], and on the ground was a one-eyed[5] alien, thumbing a ride. She [6]planned either[6] to stay on Earth awhile or had other means of returning home. I stopped.

"The alien was soon settled into my car[7] her case balanced carefully on her lap. She said her name was 'Aaarveugh',[8] which, in English, is Doris. She was very similar to we[9] humans[10] with some exceptions. She had the extra eye, and she had much better visual dexterity than us[11]. She could see in any direction[12], individually or in a group, by swivelling the eye stems[12].

"[13]How would you like to have my visual abilities?[13] she queried. I was interested.

"'We have identified the gene site for the trait, and it is on the X chromosome. If you drink a bottle of the chromosomes and special enzymes, you can be sure that the gene will attach itself to your DNA.' It sounded great, but I wondered if there was a catch?[14] There was.

"'We have heard of the numerous lawyers, as well as the great interest in self-improvement, here on Earth. In return for a vial, you must do several things: find a patent attorney for me; ingest the chromosomes, along with the enzymes,[15] and demonstrate the results to fellow humans. We will market this product extensively.'

"The alien and me[16] made a pact; she rummaged between[17] the bottles and selected one for me.

"I have agreed to spread the word about these special bottles to you, my fellow Hoax Masters. I'm sure you'll all want one now that you've heard my story of the 'X vials.'[18]

Thaddeus concluded his presentation by sweeping his eyes 360 degrees around the room.

1. *June* '99—Punctuation: comma unnecessary between month and year [**5.41 a**]
2. June *'99*—Punctuation: apostrophe replaces numerals in year [**5.1**]
3. *I* met—Usage: dangling modifier [**4.16**]
   (Acceptable: *while I was driving*, my eyes…)
4. *south*—Content: see caption [**2.1**]
5. *three-eyed*—Content: see illustration [**2.1**]
6. *either planned*—Usage: correlative conjunctions (*either/or*) each followed by parallel phrase [**4.13**]
7. *car, her*—Punctuation: comma used with absolute phrase [**5.32**]
8. *'Aaarveugh,'*—Punctuation: comma used inside quotation marks [**5.40**]
9. *us*—Grammar: pronoun used as object [**3.22**]
10. *humans,*—Punctuation: comma used to avoid ambiguity [**5.36**]
11. than *we*—Grammar: pronoun following *than* in incomplete construction [**3.24**]
12. *direction by swivelling the eye stems, individually or in a group.*—Usage: misplaced modifier [**4.15**]
    (Acceptable: *direction by swivelling, individually or in a group, the eye stems.*)
13. *"'How …abilities?'*—Punctuation: single quotation marks enclose quote within quote [**5.65**]
14. *catch.*—Punctuation: question mark unnecessary after indirect question [**5.57**]
15. *enzymes*;—Punctuation: semicolon separates clauses in a series containing commas [**5.70**]
16. alien and *I*—Grammar: pronoun used as subject [**3.22**]
17. *among*—Usage: word pair (between/among) [**4.18**]
18. *vials.'"*—Punctuation: quotation marks after final paragraph of quote spanning several paragraphs [**5.62**]

A Patent Lie? Corrected

Thaddeus related the following story at the June '99 Hoax Masters Club meeting:

"Driving home last week, I met with an unusual sight: a huge saucer was spinning south, and on the ground was a three-eyed alien, thumbing a ride. She either planned to stay on Earth awhile or had other means of returning home. I stopped.

"The alien was soon settled into my car, her case balanced carefully on her lap. She said her name was 'Aaarveugh,' which, in English, is Doris. She was very similar to us humans, with some exceptions. She had the extra eye, and she had much better visual dexterity than we. She could see in any direction by swivelling the eye stems, individually or in a group.

"'How would you like to have my visual abilities?'" she queried. I was interested.

"'We have identified the gene site for the trait, and it is on the X chromosome. If you drink a bottle of the chromosomes and special enzymes, you can be sure that the gene will attach itself to your DNA.' It sounded great, but I wondered if there was a catch. There was.

"'We have heard of the numerous lawyers, as well as the great interest in self-improvement, here on Earth. In return for a vial, you must do several things: find a patent attorney for me; ingest the chromosomes, along with the enzymes; and demonstrate the results to fellow humans. We will market this product extensively.'

"The alien and I made a pact; she

rummaged among the bottles and selected one for me.

"I have agreed to spread the word about these special bottles to you, my fellow Hoax Masters. I'm sure you'll all want one now that you've heard my story of the 'X vials.'"

Thaddeus concluded his presentation by sweeping his eyes 360 degrees around the room.

GUIDE TO GRAMMAR, USAGE, AND PUNCTUATION

The punctuation, grammar, and usage guidelines that follow cover all the skills used in this book. These skills represent an advanced-level English curriculum. This guide is not meant to be a complete English reference but rather an aid in improving written and spoken English.

The types of errors are broken down into these areas: capitalization, content, grammar, usage, punctuation, and spelling.

CAPITALIZATION

1.1 Capitalize the first word in a sentence.

> What a day we had!

1.2 Capitalize the first word in a direct quote. Do not capitalize the first word in the second half of a divided quotation or the first word of a sentence fragment.

> Jose said, "Come and look at the beautiful new mural on display in the library."
>
> "Come," Jose said, "and look at the beautiful new mural on display in the library."
>
> Jose said that he wanted us to see "the beautiful new mural."

1.3 Capitalize the first word of a statement or question within a sentence.

> The question is, Will he be able to complete the project?
>
> Always remember, What goes up must come down.

1.4 Use a capital letter for a proper noun. A proper noun names a specific person, place, or thing. (In general, a noun that is not proper should be lower case.)

> Paris, France   the World Series   John Doe

1.5 Use a capital letter for a proper adjective. A proper adjective is derived from a proper noun. (In general, an adjective that is not proper should be lower case.)

> French cooking   African tribes   a Southern accent

1.6 Do not capitalize compass directions unless they refer to a specific recognized region. (A clue is that specific regions are often preceded by *the*.)

> We are going south this summer.   We are going to the South this summer.
>
> We are headed west.   We are visiting the West Coast.

1.7 Use a capital letter on the abbreviated form of proper nouns and proper adjectives.

> Nov. 27   U.C.L.A.

1.8 Use a capital letter on titles and their abbreviated forms when they are used as part of a name or in place of a name. However, do not capitalize titles when they are not used as part of a name or in place of a name.

Captain John Smith John Smith was the captain.

Yes, Captain, the lieutenant left at noon.

Dr. Susan White We saw the doctor.

Oh, Doctor, how much of this medicine do I take?

Astronomer Lowell Mr. Lowell, noted astronomer.

We spoke with noted astronomer Percival Lowell.

Usage note: Beware of a tendency to overcapitalize. Many people want to capitalize titles regardless of their position. As a rule of thumb, if you can replace the title with the person's name (or if the title precedes the name and is used as part of it), then it is appropriate to capitalize the title.

1.9 Capitalize academic degrees when they follow a name.

Susan White, M.D. James Herriott, D.V.M. Rita MacIntyre, Ph.D.

1.10 Capitalize words of familial relation only when used in place of a name.

At 1:00, Mother called us in for lunch.

My mother called us in for lunch.

1.11 Capitalize the days of the week, the months, and the holidays.

Monday, December 24 New Year's Day

1.12 Capitalize a season only when it is being personified.

autumn leaves summer vacation as Winter grasped us in its chilly hands

1.13 Do not capitalize school subjects (except for proper nouns or adjectives) unless they are followed by a course number.

American history chemistry algebra

French British Literature II Algebra 2A

1.14 Always capitalize the first and last words in titles of books, stories, articles, movies, paintings, and other works of art. Capitalize all other words except for articles (*a, an, the*), coordinating conjunctions (*and, but, or, nor*), prepositions of five letters or fewer (*in, with, on,* etc.), and the *to* in infinitives.

For Whom the Bell Tolls *In the Heat of the Night* *Gone with the Wind*

Noodlehead Stories from Around the World *Hansel and Gretel*

Love Is a Many Splendored Thing *How to Succeed in Business*

Usage note: Style manuals disagree about capitalizing prepositions in titles. More conservative manuals say that prepositions should not be capitalized regardless of length (unless they are the first or last word in the title). The trend, however, seems to be toward capitalizing the longer prepositions (*through, around,* etc.) and leaving shorter prepositions lower case. The cutoff in length seems to be around five letters, and you will see prepositions like *under* styled both upper case and lower case.

CONTENT 2.1 In *Editor in Chief*®, content errors occur only where the story contradicts the caption or illustration, which are correct. Some content errors will be simple differences in information between an illustration/caption and the story. Other content errors will require the student to analyze information from the illustration/caption in order to correct the paragraph.

Note: There has been a trend toward dropping the negative in the expression "couldn't care less" ("could care less"); the resulting expression means the opposite of what is usually intended. (If I *could* care less, then I must already care.)

GRAMMAR   Parts of Speech

Adjectives and Adverbs

Both adjectives and adverbs modify (give information about) other words and, hence, are referred to by the general term "modifiers."

Adjectives

3.1   Adjectives tell what kind (*small* house), which one (*new* hat), or how many (*one* child). Adjectives modify nouns or pronouns. See "Problems with Modifiers," p. 113, for more information.

3.2   The demonstrative adjectives *this* and *these* are used to indicate something that is nearby, while *that* and *those* are used to indicate something that is farther away.

> Nearby: *this* house, *these* houses
>
> Farther away: *that* house, *those* houses

3.3   Here and there are unnecessary with *this, that, these,* and *those.*

> Incorrect: this here box
>
> Correct: this box

See "Comparing and Contrasting Adjectives and Adverbs," p. 85, for more information on using adjectives. See "Demonstrative Pronouns," p. 93, for more on *this, that, these,* and *those.* See "Participle as Verbal," p. 103, for information on participles as adjectives.

Adverbs

3.4   Adverbs modify verbs, adjectives, or other adverbs. Adverbs tell how, when, where, how often, how much, or to what extent. Regular adverbs are formed by adding *-ly* to an adjective; however, not all words that end in *-ly* are adverbs, and not all adverbs end in *-ly.*

> Example: She ran *quickly*. (*quickly* modifies verb—tells how she ran)
>
> Example: I swam *yesterday*. (*yesterday* modifies verb—tells when I swam)
>
> Example: He walked *downtown*. (downtown modifies verb—tells where he walked)

Example: It is *very rarely* hot here. (very modifies adverb; rarely modifies adjective—together they tell how often it is hot)

Example: That is an *extremely* beautiful apple. (extremely modifies adjective—tells to what extent the apple is beautiful)

See "Comparing and Contrasting Adjectives and Adverbs" below for more on using adverbs.

Articles

3.5   Articles (a, an, the) are adjectives. Use *an* before a vowel sound, *a* before a consonant sound. Confusion over which article to use most often comes with words beginning in *h*. If the word clearly begins with a vowel or consonant sound, the standard rule for articles applies. Confusion usually comes in words beginning with *h* in which the *h* is part of an unstressed or lightly stressed first syllable. In such cases, it is considered acceptable to use either *a* or *an*.

Examples: an hour, a ham

Examples: a historian or an historian, a heroic or an heroic

Comparative and Superlative Forms of Adjectives and Adverbs

3.6   Comparative and superlative forms of adjectives and adverbs are used to compare the degrees of characteristics possessed by the objects that they modify.

Most one-syllable adjectives/adverbs add the suffix *-er* or *-est* to the positive form.

hot—hotter—hottest   small—smaller—smallest
lucky—luckier—luckiest

Some adjectives/adverbs use *more/most* to create the comparative and superlative forms.

quietly—more quietly—most quietly
beautiful—more beautiful—most beautiful
difficult—more difficult—most difficult

Less and *least* can also be used to create comparative and superlative forms. (Note that in some modifiers, the base word is unaltered.)

aggressive—less aggressive—least aggressive
powerful—less powerful—least powerful

Irregular comparative forms

good/well—better—best

bad—worse—worst

many/much—more—most

Whether you use the comparative or superlative form depends on how many things are being compared.

Comparative: The comparative form of adjectives and adverbs is used when comparing two things.

He is the *older* of two children. (adjective)

The Jets are *better* than the Eagles. (adjective)

She runs *faster* than the boys. (adverb) *Note that she is not part of the boys.*

Superlative: The superlative form is used when comparing more than two things.

He is the *oldest* child of seven. (adjective)

The Jets are the *sharpest* of all the teams. (adjective)

She is the *best* player on the team. (adjective) *Note that she is part of the team.*

He sings the *most beautifully*. (adverb)

Comparing and Contrasting Adjectives and Adverbs

3.7   Most (but not all) adverbs end in *-ly*. Adjectives usually don't end in *-ly* (although a few do). Sometimes the same word functions as an adjective and an adverb. Sometimes adverbs of a particular word have more than one form. See the examples below.

Adjective	Adverb	Adverb ending in *-ly*
a *high* window	He leaped *high*.	We think *highly* of him.
a *close* encounter	He walked *close* to her.	We watched her *closely*.

Adjective ending in *-ly*	Adverb
nightly train	We go *nightly*.
lively tune	Step *lively*, boys!

These examples show that distinguishing between adverbs and adjectives is not as simple as checking to see whether a word ends in *-ly*. You need to see what the word modifies (describes).

Adjectives modify	Adverbs modify
nouns	verbs
pronouns	adjectives
	other adverbs

Adjective: It rained *last* night. (*last* tells which night; it modifies the noun *night*)

Adverb: Our team played *last*. (*last* tells when the team played; it modifies the verb *played*)

Linking verbs are frequently followed by adjectives.

Adjective: She looked *pretty*. (*pretty* modifies the subject she)

Adjective: He sounded *happy*. (*happy* modifies the subject he)

Adjective: He felt *bad*. (*bad* modifies the subject he)

Many verbs that function as linking verbs can also be used as action verbs. In these cases, the action verbs will be followed by adverbs rather than adjectives.

Linking verb with adjective: He stayed *quiet*. (*quiet* modifies the subject he)

Action verb with adverb: He stayed *quietly* in his seat. (*quietly* modifies the verb stayed; it tells how he stayed in his seat)

Linking verbs take adjectives. Action verbs take adverbs. See "Linking Verbs," p. 102.

Coordinate and Noncoordinate Modifiers

3.8   Two or more adjectives or adverbs can combine to modify a word or phrase. The exact relationship between the modifiers and the word they modify is conveyed by punctuation: coordinate modifiers are separated by commas, noncoordinate modifiers do not take any punctuation.

3.9   **Coordinate modifiers:** Coordinate modifiers are two (or more) adjectives or adverbs that equally and separately modify a word or phrase. To determine if the modifiers are coordinate, insert *and* between the modifiers and listen to how the sentence sounds or reverse the order of the modifiers and see if the meaning remains the same. If the sentence still works with these changes, then the modifiers are coordinate modifiers.

> Coordinate adjectives: She was a loyal, conscientious person.
>
> Test: She was a loyal *and* conscientious person. She was a conscientious, loyal person.
>
> Coordinate adverbs: The seal swam smoothly, gracefully through the water.
>
> Test: The seal swam smoothly *and* gracefully through the water. The seal swam gracefully, smoothly through the water.

Coordinate modifiers are separated by commas.

3.10   **Noncoordinate adjectives:** Adjectives are noncoordinate when one adjective modifies the noun plus the adjective that immediately precedes the noun; for example, in the phrase "the first spring flower," *first* and *spring* do not modify flower in the same way. *First* modifies the noun (flower) plus the adjective that immediately precedes it (spring); that is, *first* modifies the combined phrase, "spring flower." We are not describing the first flower or the first spring, but the first flower of spring. Some examples of noncoordinate adjectives are listed below.

> big orange cat (*big* modifies orange cat)
>
> chewy oatmeal cookies (*chewy* modifies oatmeal cookies)
>
> excellent football player (*excellent* modifies football player)

You can use the test for coordinate modifiers to help recognize noncoordinate modifiers. If you make the test changes and the sentence no longer has the same meaning, then the modifiers are noncoordinate.

> Test "big orange cat": big *and* orange cat; orange big cat
>
> Test "chewy oatmeal cookies": chewy *and* oatmeal cookies; oatmeal chewy cookies
>
> Test "excellent football player": excellent *and* football player; football excellent player

The tests show that the first adjective is modifying the noun plus the adjective immediately preceding the noun.

There should be no punctuation between noncoordinate adjectives.

Compound Adjectives

3.11   Compound adjectives are unit modifiers, words that work together as a unit to modify a noun or pronoun; for example, when we say "a quick-thinking speaker" we do not mean a quick speaker or a thinking speaker, but a speaker who thinks quickly. Although compound adjectives function as adjectives, they may be composed of not only adjectives but also adverbs, nouns, participles, and even verbs. Some examples of compound adjectives are listed below.

high-risk ventures	more-organized approach	fleece-lined coat
all-out effort	well-documented complaint	much-loved pet
blue-green algae	better-known candidate	50-yard dash

Phrases may also function as compound adjectives.

a spur-of-the-moment decision   how-to books   a face-the-facts meeting

To prevent confusion and to ease reading, compound adjectives are generally hyphenated when they immediately precede the noun that they modify. The example below demonstrates how meaning can differ with and without the hyphen.

He will be satisfied only with some more intricate plans. (He already has some intricate plans but wants more of them.)

He will be satisfied only with some more-intricate plans. (He has some plans but wants some that are more intricate.)

Compound adjectives that are so well known that misreading is unlikely are rarely hyphenated.

high school classes	sodium chloride solution	blood pressure cuff
Civil War stories	per capita income	dry goods store

Note that when an adverb ending in *-ly* modifies an adjective that is modifying a noun, no punctuation falls between the adverb and the adjective, as adverb + adjective + noun is the normal word order.

a highly disputed case   an overly anxious manner   the widely held opinion

In some cases, compound adjectives are also hyphenated when acting as a predicate adjective (following a linking verb) if they still function as a unit modifier.

That dog is good-looking.   He seems tough-minded.

See also "Coordinate and Noncoordinate Modifiers," p. 85, for more information.

Participles Used as Adjectives

3.12   The present or past participle forms of verbs can be used as adjectives to modify nouns or pronouns. In the examples below, the same participle is shown used as an adjective and as a part of the verb. (In the latter case, the verb phrase is *be* + participle.)

Adjective—present participle: The *crying* child ran to his mother. (*crying* modifies child)

Verb phrase—present participle: The child was *crying* as he ran to his mother. (*was crying* is the verb phrase)

Adjective—past participle: The *tired* child ran to his mother. (*tired* modifies child)

Verb phrase—past participle: The child had *tired* himself by running to his mother. (*had tired* is the verb phrase)

See "Participle as Verb," pp. 102–103, for more on participles as verbs.

Well/Good

3.13   As modifiers, *well* and *good* are sometimes a source of confusion. *Well* is both an adverb and an adjective while *good* is only an adjective. Perhaps some of the confusion comes because *well* and *good* occasionally overlap in meaning. You can say either "He feels well" or "He feels good" to indicate a general state of health. *Good* is not limited to describing health, however. You can say, "He feels good about his promotion." *Well* cannot be used in this way. As an adjective, *well* has only three meanings:

1. to be healthy

   He looks *well*.

2. to look well-dressed or well-groomed

   He looks *well* in a suit.

3. to be satisfactory, right, or proper

   It is *well* to fulfill your commitments.

Good, on the other hand, is always an adjective. It cannot be used to modify a verb. In the examples below, *well* and *good* convey similar meanings, but they do so by modifying different types of words.

Good: You did a *good* job. (*good* is an adjective; it modifies job)

Well: You did *well*. (*well* is an adverb; it modifies did)

Another source of confusion may be that the comparative and superlative forms are the same for *good* and *well*: good, better, best and well, better, best. See "Comparative and Superlative Forms of Adjectives and Adverbs," p. 84.

Conjunctions

     The word *conjunction* refers to joining or coming together. We use conjunctions to join various grammatical elements: words, phrases, clauses. There are three kinds of conjunctions: coordinating, correlative, and subordinating. Each of these three types of conjunctions is described below.

Coordinating Conjunctions

3.14   Coordinating conjunctions join words, phrases, clauses, or sentences. The word *coordinating* indicates that the elements that are joined have equal grammatical weight—for example, nouns with other nouns, verbs with other verbs, clauses with other clauses of equal rank.

He *ran and jumped*. (verb with verb)

We could use a new *car or truck*. (noun with noun)

I saw *two of my friends but none of my relatives* at the wedding. (2 phrases)

She had a new computer, so she took a class on home computing. (2 independent clauses)

There are seven coordinating conjunctions. To assist in remembering these conjunctions, use their first letters to form a mnemonic aid:

FAN BOYS—**f**or, **a**nd, **n**or, **b**ut, **o**r, **y**et, **s**o. *And, but, or,* and *nor* are always used as coordinating conjunctions; *for, yet,* and *so* do not always function as coordinating conjunctions. In fact, *for* and *yet* are rarely used as conjunctions. Use the tricks below to decide whether *for, yet,* and *so* are functioning as conjunctions.

For usually functions as a preposition and is often found at the beginning of prepositional phrases. When *for* can be replaced by the word *because, for* is functioning as a conjunction.

> Preposition: We are going home *for* lunch.
>
> Conjunction: We are going home, *for* lunch is served at 1:00. (*for* means because)

Yet usually functions as an adverb referring to time. When *yet* can be replaced by *but* or *nevertheless,* it is functioning as a conjunction.

> Adverb: We are not *yet* ready to go.
>
> Conjunction: We are not ready, *yet* we will go. (*yet* means but)

So usually functions as an adverb that intensifies the word it modifies. *So* is also commonly used as shorthand for *so that* (a subordinating conjunction). When *so* can be replaced by *thus* or *therefore,* it is functioning as a coordinating conjunction.

> Adverb: That dog is *so* strong.
>
> Subordinating conjunction: We need a strong dog *so* he can pull our sled. (*so* is short for so that)
>
> Coordinating conjunction: That dog is strong, *so* we used him to pull our sled. (*so* means therefore)

Note that in the examples above, when *for, yet,* and *so* function as coordinating conjunctions, they are preceded by commas. When a coordinating conjunction joins two independent clauses, or main clauses, the conjunction should be preceded by a comma unless the independent clauses are short and closely related.

> We went to Paris, but we stayed only a few days.
>
> He came and he went.

See "Parallel Structure," p. 112, for more on using coordinating conjunctions.

Correlative Conjunctions

3.15   Correlative conjunctions is the name given to conjunctions used in pairs. The following are common correlative conjunctions:

> either...or   neither...nor   both...and   not only...but (also)
> whether...or

As with coordinating conjunctions, correlative conjunctions join elements of similar grammatical construction, e.g., two adjectives, two prepositional phrases, two independent clauses, etc. Another way to think of this is that correlative conjunctions join constructions that are parallel. Correlative conjunctions should be placed as close as possible to the elements they join.

Misplaced: Either *we will go to the lake* or *to the seashore.* (joins independent clause and prepositional phrase)

Correct: We will go either *to the lake* or *to the seashore.* (joins 2 prepositional phrases)

In general, correlative conjunctions do not require commas; however, they may need a comma if they join two independent clauses. In the first example below, *not only...but* joins two independent clauses. In the second example, the same correlative conjunction joins two nouns (*cat* and *dog*).

Not only do we have to wash the car, but we also must shampoo the carpets.

We have not only a cat but also a dog.

Subordinating Conjunctions

3.16   Subordinating conjunctions join subordinate, or dependent, clauses to independent clauses. The following are commonly used subordinating conjunctions:

after	before	since	when
although	even though	so that	whenever
as	how	than	where
as if	if	that	wherever
as though	in order that	though	whether
as much as	inasmuch as	unless	while
because	provided	until	

Anytime a subordinating conjunction begins a clause, that clause will be a subordinate clause. This is true even if the clause that follows the conjunction would otherwise be an independent clause.

Independent clause: we left the party

Subordinate (dependent) clause: after we left the party

Some of the subordinating conjunctions also function as other parts of speech: *after, as, before, once, since,* and *until* sometimes function as prepositions; *how, when,* and *where* can be adverbs; *that* is often a relative or demonstrative pronoun. To determine whether one of these words is functioning as a subordinating conjunction or some other part of speech, remember first that subordinating conjunctions join words or groups of words.

Adverb: *How* does he do it?

Subordinating conjunction: We don't know *how* he does it.

Relative pronoun: *That* dog was so large.

Subordinating conjunction: We did not know *that* the dog was so large.

It would be easy if a subordinating conjunction always had to be in the middle of the words it joins; however, subordinating conjunctions can begin sentences. Prepositions also frequently begin sentences. To distinguish between a preposition and a subordinating conjunction, look for the first noun or pronoun that follows the word in question. If that noun or pronoun is the subject of a clause, then the word in question is a subordinating conjunction. If the noun or pronoun is not the subject of a clause, the word is a preposition. In other words, the second clue to remember is that subordinating conjunctions always begin clauses, not phrases.

> Preposition: *Before* the meeting, we want to get coffee. (*meeting* is not the subject of a clause)
>
> Subordinating conjunction: *Before* the meeting begins, we want to get coffee. (*meeting* is the subject of a clause, "the meeting begins")

3.17   **Commas with dependent clauses:** In general, when a sentence consists of a dependent clause followed by an independent clause, the dependent clause should be followed by a comma.

> Dependent clause + independent clause: After we left the party, we went for a walk.
>
> Dependent clause + independent clause: While the neighbors were away, the dog dug up the roses.

In general, when a dependent clause follows an independent clause, no comma is required.

> Independent clause + dependent clause: We went for a walk after we left the party.
>
> Independent clause + dependent clause: The dog dug up the roses while the neighbors were away.

Beginning writers often insert commas before clauses beginning with the conjunctions *since* and *because*. *Since* and *because*, however, are subordinating, not coordinating, conjunctions. This means that even if *since* or *because* is followed by an independent clause, that clause is made subordinate by *since* or *because*. Such sentences containing *since* or *because* are examples of independent clauses + dependent clauses and do not require a comma.

> Example: We went right home from the store because we were afraid the ice cream would melt.
>
> Example: I wanted to ask him about the football game since I knew he had seen it.

For more on independent and dependent clauses, see "Clauses," p. 105, and "Clauses and Punctuation," p. 127.

3.18   **Essential and nonessential clauses:** Essential (restrictive) and nonessential (nonrestrictive) dependent clauses compose a special subcategory of dependent clauses. As their names imply, essential clauses are essential to the meaning of a sentence. Nonessential clauses are not essential to the meaning of a sentence. Nonessential clauses can be removed from a sentence without altering the basic meaning of the sentence.

As an example of the essential clause, consider the following: We want to point out a male friend who is standing with a number of other men, so we need to give some information that will help our audience to identify the specific man we are referring to. We mention that the man is wearing a red hat as an aid in identifying him. The sentence would read as shown below.

> Essential: The man who is wearing a red hat is a friend of mine.

As an example of the nonessential clause, consider the following: We want to point out the same male friend, but this time there are no other men near him. We mention that he is wearing a red hat, but we are not using that fact as a means to identify him; we just add the information about the hat for a bit of interest.

> Nonessential: That man, who is wearing a red hat, is a friend of mine.

In the examples above, the dependent clause "who is wearing a red hat" functions as an essential or a nonessential clause depending upon the meaning of the sentence. Commas are needed if the clause is nonessential; however, if the clause is essential to the meaning of the sentence, commas are not used. Consider the examples below.

> Nonessential: Jason, who always gets into trouble, broke the vase.
> Essential: The brother who always gets into trouble broke the vase.

In the first example above, we know that Jason broke the vase. The clause set off by commas gives us more information about Jason, but we do not need that information to identify him. In the second example, however, the clause "who always gets into trouble" tells us which brother it was who broke the vase; therefore, this clause is essential.

See "Clauses and Punctuation," p. 127, for more on essential and nonessential clauses.

Pronouns

A pronoun is used in place of a noun or nouns (antecedent) to which the pronoun refers.

Clear Reference

3.19   When using a pronoun, make certain that the antecedent of the pronoun is clear. Unless the reader knows to what noun or nouns a pronoun is referring, the sentence becomes meaningless or confusing. For example, "She saw them" has no meaning without knowing to which "she" and "them" the sentence refers.

Ambiguous reference: If a pronoun has more than one possible antecedent, change the sentence so that the reference of the pronoun is unmistakably clear. Sometimes the sentence can be made clear by substituting a noun for the pronoun, but in other cases, the sentence must be rewritten. Ambiguous reference can be a particular problem with the pronouns *this, that, these, those, they, them,* and *it.*

> Unclear: After the dogs made muddy footprints on the floors, she was obliged to clean them. (the dogs or the floors?)

Rephrased: After the dogs made muddy footprints on the floors, she was obliged to clean the floors.

Unclear: Our sons played with the neighbor's children before they went to their swimming lesson. (who went to the lesson?)

Rephrased: Before our sons went to their swimming lesson, they played with the neighbor's children.

General reference: Avoid using pronouns to refer to general ideas or to replace a series of general statements. General reference can be a particular problem with the pronouns *which*, *this*, *that*, and *it*.

Unclear: Our neighbor allows her cat on the kitchen counters which we disapprove of.

Rephrased: We disapprove of our neighbor's allowing her cat on the kitchen counters.

Unclear: We went to the beach, rented a boat, capsized, and waited the rest of the day for rescue. It was not what I had expected.

Rephrased: We went to the beach, rented a boat, capsized, and waited the rest of the day for rescue. Our day at the beach was not what I had expected.

Unclear: He forgot that the bank would be closed for the holiday. This caused him some difficulty.

Rephrased: He forgot that the bank would be closed for the holiday. This oversight caused him some difficulty.

Since *this* is one of the worst culprits for general reference, a good rule of thumb is to avoid using *this* alone. In other words, use *this* as an adjective (*this* event, *this* idea) rather than as a demonstrative pronoun. See "Demonstrative Pronouns" below.

Demonstrative Pronouns

3.20   When used alone (not modifying a noun), *this*, *that*, *these*, and *those* function as nouns and are considered demonstrative pronouns.

This is a very nice rug.

Those are pretty flowers.

In addition to identifying people or things, the demonstrative pronouns can be used to indicate spatial relationships.

This is my house; *that* is my sister's. (*This* one is nearby; *that* one is farther away.)

Indefinite Pronouns

3.21   An indefinite pronoun does not refer to a specific person or thing. Some common indefinite pronouns are listed below.

all	each	much	other
another	each one	most	several
any	either	neither	some
anybody	everybody	nobody	somebody
anyone	everyone	none	someone
anything	few	no one	somthing
both	many	one	such

Indefinite pronouns are often used to make general statements or to indicate quantity.

Everybody knows how upset she was.

Most of the band members showed up for practice.

Unlike personal pronouns, indefinite pronouns use an apostrophe and *s* to form the possessive.

Everyone's cars got muddy after the storm.

He felt that *one's* actions should reflect *one's* beliefs.

Note that if the indefinite pronoun is used as a possessive with *else*, *else* takes the apostrophe and *s*.

No one else's project looked as good as hers.

Personal Pronouns

3.22   A personal pronoun replaces a noun or nouns. The pronoun must always agree in number and gender with the noun or nouns it replaces. Pronouns may be used as subjects or objects in a sentence. When a pronoun is used as the subject in a sentence, the verb must agree with the pronoun in number. Pronouns may also show possession. A possessive pronoun may be used before a noun to show possession (*my* bike), or a possessive pronoun may stand alone. (The bike is *mine*.) See the chart below.

Confusion in pronoun usage frequently occurs with compound subjects or objects (she and I, him and me). The easiest way to determine the correct form of the pronoun is to look at each member of the compound subject or object separately, as in these examples:

Marla and I went home. (*Marla* went home. *I* went home.)

Kim Lee went with him and me. (Kim Lee went with *him*. Kim Lee went with *me*.)

Bruce and he saw the movie. (*Bruce* saw the movie. *He* saw the movie.)

When the compound subject is broken apart in this way, most native speakers will recognize the correct pronoun form.

Note that in the examples above the first person pronouns (I, me; we, us) always appear last in compound subjects and objects.

SINGULAR/ PLURAL	PERSON	NOMINATIVE CASE (SUBJECT)	OBJECTIVE CASE (OBJECT)	POSSESSIVE CASE	
				BEFORE NOUN	STANDING ALONE
singular	first person	I	me	my	mine
singular	second person	you	you	your	yours
singular	third person	he	him	his	his
singular	third person	she	her	her	hers
singular	third person	it	it	its	its
plural	first person	we	us	our	ours
plural	second person	you	you	your	yours
plural	third person	they	them	their	theirs

Confusion may also occur regarding the correct pronoun to use after *than* or *as* (see below). In such constructions, part of the phrase is implied. By completing the phrase, the proper pronoun to use becomes clear.

He runs faster than I. (faster than I do)

She is not as old as he. (as he is)

Sometimes using the correct pronoun is absolutely essential to the meaning of the sentence. Consider the examples below.

He likes frogs better than she. (better than she does)

He likes frogs better than her. (better than he likes her)

Predicate Nominative

3.23   Although "It's me" has become commonly accepted in informal English, it is still not considered proper in formal (especially formal *written*) English. In formal English, the old saying "*Be* takes the nominative" still holds true.

Nominative refers to the "case" of the pronoun. Pronouns take different forms depending on their function in a sentence. These different functions and the forms that correspond to those functions are known as "cases." Subjects are in the nominative case, objects are in the objective case, and nouns and pronouns that show possession are in the possessive case. See "Personal Pronouns," p. 94, for examples of pronouns used as subjects, objects, and possessives.

When a pronoun follows any of the forms of the verb *to be* and refers to the subject, the pronoun is called a predicate nominative and should be in the nominative case (the "subject case").

It was I.

I am she.

It will be he who wins the award.

Pronouns in Incomplete Constructions

3.24   Incomplete constructions are constructions in which some of the words are implied rather than stated. Such constructions occur most frequently after *as* and *than* and often involve a pronoun.

Can he teach her as well as me? (can he teach both of us?)

Can he teach her as well as I? (can he teach as well as I can?)

In the examples above, the meanings of the sentences differ with the pronouns used. To determine which pronoun to use, imagine completing the clause.

He likes frogs better than she. (better than she likes frogs)

He likes frogs better than her. (better than he likes her)

Reflexive and Intensive Pronouns

3.25   Reflexive and intensive pronouns use the same form. They are pronouns that end in *-self* or *-selves*: myself, yourself, herself, himself, itself, ourselves, yourselves, and themselves. They are used to refer to (reflexive) or emphasize (intensive) another noun or pronoun within the sentence.

Reflexive: A reflexive pronoun "reflects" back on an antecedent (the noun or pronoun to which it refers) that is within the same sentence.

> Reflexive: I went by *myself*. (antecedent = I)
>
> Reflexive: We could have done that *ourselves*. (antecedent = we)

Intensive: An intensive pronoun is used to emphasize or intensify an antecedent that is within the same sentence.

> Intensive: The girls *themselves* thought of the idea. (antecedent = the girls)
>
> Intensive: You *yourself* may have seen something similar. (antecedent = you)

Note that both reflexive and intensive pronouns must have an antecedent that is within the same sentence. There is sometimes a tendency to use these pronouns incorrectly in place of personal pronouns.

> Incorrect: She and *myself* went to the store after school. (no antecedent for *myself* in this sentence)
>
> Correct: She and *I* went to the store after school.
>
> Incorrect: He went with *myself*. (no antecedent for *myself* in this sentence)
>
> Correct: He went with *me*.

Relative Pronouns: Who and Whom

3.26   The relative pronouns have different forms depending upon their function in the sentence: subject, object, or possessive.

SUBJECT (Nominative Case)	OBJECT (Objective Case)	POSSESSIVE (Possessive Case)
who	whom	whose
whoever	whomever	whosoever

Confusion often arises over whether to use *who* or *whom*. If the relative pronoun functions as the subject, use who; if it functions as the object, use whom. The difficulty often lies in deciding whether you need a subject or an object.

> Subject: Who is coming for dinner?
>
> Object: Whom are we waiting for?

The easiest way to decide whether to use *who* or *whom* is to mentally drop *who / whom* and the words preceding it and determine whether you can make a sentence with the words that are left by adding *he* or *him*. If you would use *he*, then the sentence needs a subject, and you should use *who*. If you would use *him*, then the sentence needs an object, and you should use *whom*.

> Sentence: Do you know who/whom will be attending the meeting?
>
> Remove who/whom: *will be attending the meeting*
>
> Add he or him: *He* will be attending the meeting.
>
> Correct: Do you know *who* will be attending the meeting?
>
> Sentence: Who/whom is the party for?
>
> Remove who/whom: *is the party for*

Add he or him: Is the party for *him*?

Correct: *Whom* is the party for?

If you are still in doubt whether to use *who* or *whom,* opt for *who.* Using *who* for *whom* may not be correct, but most people won't notice. Using *whom* for *who,* on the other hand, sounds pretentious.

Verbs

Verb Parts

3.27   All verbs have four principal parts: infinitive (sometimes called "plain verb"), present participle, past, and past participle. Present and past participles are used with helping verbs to form verb phrases. Regular verbs form the past and past participle by adding *-d* or *-ed* to the infinitive. Irregular verbs form the past and past participle forms in a different way, such as by changing spelling or by not changing at all.

Regular Verbs

Infinitive	Present Participle	Past	Past Participle
care	caring	cared	cared
call	calling	called	called
jump	jumping	jumped	jumped
walk	walking	walked	walked

Irregular Verbs

Infinitive	Present Participle	Past	Past Participle
become	becoming	became	become
bring	bringing	brought	brought
choose	choosing	chose	chosen
go	going	went	gone
ride	riding	rode	ridden
think	thinking	thought	thought
pay	paying	paid	paid
know	knowing	know	known
shrink	shrinking	shrank (or shrunk)	shrunk (or shrunken)

Verb Phrase

3.28   A verb phrase consists of a main verb and one or more helping verbs (also called auxiliary verbs). A few verb phrases follow:

has gone   is going   will have gone   will be going

Since many verb phrases are formed using the verb *to be,* we review its parts below:

Infinitive	Present Participle	Past	Past Participle
be	being	was, were	been

Tense	Part of Verb Used	Example
present tense	Active: infinitive	Active: I ask.
	(Passive: be + past participle)	(Passive: I am asked.)
present progressive	be + present participle	I am asking.
present emphatic	do + infinitive	I do ask.
present perfect tense	have or has + past participle	I have asked.
present perfect progressive	have or has + be (past participle) + present participle	I have been asking.
past tense	Active: past	Active: I asked.
	(Passive: be [past] and past participle)	(Passive: I was asked.)
past progressive	be (past) + present participle	I was asking.
past emphatic	do (past) + infinitive	I did ask.
past perfect tense	had + past participle	I had asked.
past perfect progressive	had + be (past participle) + present participle	I had been asking.
future tense	Active: will or shall + infinitive	Active: I will ask.
	(Passive: will or shall + be + past participle)	(Passive: I will be asked.)
future progressive	will or shall + be (infinitive) + present participle	I will be asking.
future perfect tense	will (or shall) have + past participle	I will have asked.
future perfect progressive	will (or shall) have + be (past participle) + present participle	I will have been asking.

Verb Tense

3.29   Tense refers to the time element expressed by a verb. Verb tense shows whether an action has already occurred, is now occurring, or will occur in the future. Although there are four principal parts to verbs, these four parts are used to form six tenses: present tense, past tense, future tense, present perfect tense, past perfect tense, and future perfect tense. These tenses can be subdivided into progressive form (*be* + present participle). Present and past can be further subdivided into emphatic. Many of these tenses (progressive, perfect, future, etc.) are formed by verb phrases rather than individual verbs. (See the table on page 99.)

Irregular verb forms are sometimes confused. For example, in the verb *do*, the simple past tense *did* is sometimes incorrectly substituted for the past participle *done* in the perfect tenses. This results in *have did* (wrong) for *have done* (right). The past participles of both *do* and *go* are always used with a helping verb to create the present perfect, the past perfect, and the future perfect tenses.

Simple Past	Perfect tenses used with past participle (shown in italics)		
did	have *done* (not did)	had *done*	will have *done*
went	have *gone* (not went)	had *gone*	will have *gone*

3.30   **Sequence of tenses:** When a sentence consists of more than one clause, the tense of the main verb affects the tenses of all other verbs

Sequence of Tenses

MAIN VERB	PRESENT				PAST				FUTURE			
	simple present	present progressive	present perfect	present perfect progressive	simple past	past progressive	past perfect	past perfect progressive	simple future	future progressive	future perfect	future perfect progressive
PRESENT TENSE I know because he…	goes home to eat.	is going home to eat.	has gone home to eat.	has been going home to eat.	went home to eat.	was going home to eat.	had gone home to eat.	had been going home to eat.	will go home to eat.	will be going home to eat.	will have gone home to eat.	will have been going home to eat.
PAST TENSE I knew because he…					went home to eat.	was going home to eat.	had gone home to eat.	had been going home to eat.	will go home to eat.	will be going home to eat.	will have gone home to eat.	will have been going home to eat.
FUTURE TENSE I will know because he…	goes home to eat.	is going home to eat.	has gone home to eat.	has been going home to eat.					will go home to eat.	will be going home to eat.	will have gone home to eat.	will have been going home to eat.

in the sentence. The tense of the main verb creates the time frame to which all the other verbs must relate. The tense of other verbs in the sentence should shift from the tense of the main verb only to convey meaning, e.g., to show the order of events.

If the main verb is in present tense, other verbs in the sentence may use any tense. Past or future tense in the main verb, however, imposes time constraints on other verbs in the sentence. For example, if the main verb is in past tense, other verbs in the sentence cannot be in present tense. If the main verb is in future tense, other verbs cannot be in the simple past tense. (See the "Sequence of Tenses" table, p. 99.)

Usage note: There is one exception to the rule that a past tense main verb should not be followed by a present tense verb in a clause. When the clause makes a statement of universal truth, the verb is in the present tense even if the main verb is in the past tense. Consider the examples below.

The teacher *taught* (past) us that a triangle *has* (present) three sides.

We *knew* (past) that he always *goes* (present) home to eat.

3.31 **Special tense problems:** Do not use *would have* in *if* clauses to express the earlier of two past actions. Use the past perfect.

Incorrect: If we would have known, we could have helped.

Correct: If we had known, we could have helped.

Use *would*, not *will*, after a past tense verb.

I *knew* this *would* happen.

Verb Mood

The "mood" of the verb helps to communicate a speaker's attitude. Verbs have three moods: imperative, indicative, and subjunctive. Imperative is used to express commands, warnings, or requests. Indicative is used to express facts or opinions or to ask a question. Subjunctive is used to express a wish or a condition contrary to fact. Subjunctive is also used in *that* clauses that express a suggestion, a demand, or a requirement.

imperative
Go to the store. (command)
I don't think you should *go* to the store. (warning)
Please *go* to the store. (request)

indicative
He *is going* to the store. (statement of fact)
I think he *is going* to the store. (opinion)
Is he *going* to the store? (question)

subjunctive
I wish I *knew* where he was. (wish)
If he *were going* to the store, he could pick up some eggs. (contrary to fact—he is not going to the store)
I suggest that he *be allowed* to go to the store. (suggestion)

I insist that he *be allowed* to go to the store. (demand)
It is essential that he *visit* the store. (requirement)

Imperative and indicative moods use the standard verb tenses. Subjunctive, however, has its own rules, as we demonstrate below.

3.32 **Subjunctive mood:** The subjunctive mood is used (1) in *that* clauses to express a demand, suggestion, or request; (2) in sentences with *wish*; and (3) in *if*, *as if*, or *as though* clauses to express something unlikely or contrary-to-fact. The subjunctive uses *were* or *be* rather than *was* or *is*, and regular verbs do not take an *s* (even with third person singular—he/she) but always use the base infinitive form.

Below, sentences are shown first in present tense subjunctive, then in past tense subjunctive. Note the way in which the verbs change in the subjunctive to show present and past time.

present tense subjunctive

I wish I *knew* the results. (*wish* takes the past tense *[knew]* to show present time)

I insist that she *be seated* by the window. (*be* is used for the verb *to be* in subjunctive *that* clauses)

We demand that she *tell* us the news. (present tense is always used in subjunctive *that* clauses)

I suggest that he *visit* his aunt. (present tense is always used in subjunctive *that* clauses; note that the verb does not take an *s*, even with *he*)

If I *were* in Hawaii, I would go surfing. (*were* shows present time)

Even if he *were* the last man on Earth, she would not go out with him. (*were* shows present time)

past tense subjunctive

I wish I *had known* the results. (*wish* takes the past perfect tense *[had known]* to show past time)

I insisted that she *be seated* by the window. (*insist* changes to past tense to show past time, *that* clause remains the same)

We demanded that she *tell* us the news. (*demand* changes to past tense to show past time, *that* clause remains the same)

I suggested that he *visit* his aunt. (*suggest* changes to past tense to show past time, *that* clause remains the same)

If I *had been* in Hawaii, I would have gone surfing. (past perfect tense shows past time)

Even if he *had been* the last man on Earth, she would not go out with him. (past perfect tense shows past time)

The subjunctive is used with *if, as if,* and *as though* clauses to show that the statement is contrary to fact.

If I *were* the manager, I would do things differently. (The speaker is not the manager.)

When we went on that new space ride, we felt as if we *were* really flying through outer space! (The speaker was not really flying.)

Although the subjunctive may seem unusual, it is in common usage in several everyday expressions: "be that as it may," "suffice it to say," "as it were," "if I were you," and "I wish I knew."

Helping Verbs

3.33   A helping verb (also called an auxiliary verb) is part of a verb phrase. A verb phrase consists of a main verb and a helping verb. Future tense, perfect tense, progressive form, and passive voice are all created using helping verbs.

Verb phrases with the helping verb marked in italics are shown below.

has written	*may* attend	*can* ski	*might have* seen
must read	*will* ride	*shall* go	*would have* taken

Common helping verbs include the following: be, can, could, do, have, may, might, must, shall, should, will, would.

Linking Verbs

3.34   Linking verbs express a state or condition rather than an action. They are called linking verbs because they link the subject to a complement which identifies or describes the subject. This subject complement may be a noun, pronoun, or adjective. Common linking verbs include the following: appear, be, become, feel, grow, look, remain, seem, smell, sound, stay, taste.

Anchovies *taste* salty.

That dog *looks* thin.

She *is* the manager.

Some linking verbs can also be used as action verbs, which can be modified by adverbs. A good way to determine whether the verb is functioning as a linking verb or action verb is to substitute the appropriate forms of *is* and *seem* for the verb. If the sentence still makes sense and has not changed its meaning, then the verb is a linking verb.

Linking verb: He remains happy. (No meaning change—He *is* happy. He *seems* happy.)

Action verb: He remains happily at the park. (Meaning changes; therefore, *remains* is not a linking verb—He *is* happily at the park. He *seems* happily at the park.)

Linking verbs take adjectives. Action verbs take adverbs.

Usage note: *Seem* is always a linking verb. When used as the main verb, *be* is a linking verb except when followed by an adverb. See "Comparing and Contrasting Adjectives and Adverbs," p. 85.

Participle as Verb: Progressive Tense vs. Passive Voice

3.35   The present participle is used with a form of the verb *be* in the progressive tense. The form of *be* determines whether the sentence is present or past progressive.

Progressive = *be* + present participle

Present progressive: The boy is flying a kite.

Past progressive: The boy was flying a kite.

The past participle is used with a form of the verb *be* in passive voice. In passive voice, the subject of the sentence is being acted upon rather than acting.

Passive voice = *be* + past participle

Passive voice (present): A kite is flown by the boy.

Passive voice (past): A kite was flown by the boy.

Of course, the past participle is also used with active voice (see examples that follow).

Participle as Verb: Examples of Usage

3.36   Examples of active and passive voice in various tenses follow.

Active (present): The dog chases the birds.

Active (present perfect): The dog has chased the birds.

Active (past): The dog chased the birds.

Active (past perfect): The dog had chased the birds.

Active (future): The dog will chase the birds.

Active (future perfect): The dog will have chased the birds.

Active (present progressive): The dog is chasing the birds.

Active (present perfect progressive): The dog has been chasing the birds.

Active (past progressive): The dog was chasing the birds.

Active (past perfect progressive): The dog had been chasing the birds.

Active (future progressive): The dog will be chasing the birds.

Active (future perfect progressive): The dog will have been chasing the birds.

Passive (present): The birds are chased by the dog.

Passive (present perfect): The birds have been chased by the dog.

Passive (past): The birds were chased by the dog.

Passive (past perfect): The birds had been chased by the dog.

Passive (future): The birds will be chased by the dog.

Passive (future perfect): The birds will have been chased by the dog.

Passive (present progressive): The birds are being chased by the dog.

Passive (past progressive): The birds were being chased by the dog.

Verbals

Verbals are formed from verbs, but although they may express action, they do not function as verbs in a sentence. Verbals function as nouns, adjectives, or adverbs. There are three types of verbals: participles, gerunds, and infinitives.

Participle as Verbal

3.37   Participles are present or past participle verb forms that function as adjectives.

Present participle: I saw the *opening* performance. (adjective)

Present participle: I saw her *running* toward the house. (adjective)

Past participle: He was proud of the *completed* project. (adjective)

Past participle: He repaired the *broken* hinge. (adjective)

Be aware that there can be some confusion when using the term *participle*. In its broadest sense, a participle is any word ending in the suffix *-ing*. In its narrowest sense, a participle is a verb form (which may or may not end in *-ing*) that functions as an adjective. The term *participle* is also used to refer to the verb forms used in the present and past progressive tenses. (See "Verb Parts," p. 97, for more on the present and past participle forms of verbs.)

See "Terminal Participles," p. 115, for more on participles.

Gerund

3.38   A gerund is a verb form ending in *-ing* (present participle) that functions as a noun.

> *Running* is her favorite hobby. (noun)
>
> She likes *skating*. (noun)

The same present participle form of a verb can serve as either a gerund (if it functions as a noun) or as a participle (if it functions as an adjective).

> Gerund: *Practicing* takes discipline. (noun)
>
> Participle: *Practicing*, she played etudes for hours. (adjective)

Infinitive

3.39   The infinitive form of a verb can be used as a noun, an adjective, or an adverb. Infinitives are usually preceded by *to,* although not always.

> We like *to ski*. (noun)
>
> She left the party *to take* a nap. (adverb)
>
> On the chair are clothes *to iron*. (adjective)

Be careful not to confuse the *to* that is part of the infinitive with the *to* used as a preposition. The infinitive is *to* + verb. The preposition is *to* + noun (or pronoun).

> infinitive: We are going *to shop*.
>
> preposition: We are going *to the store*.

3.40   **Split infinitives:** Splitting an infinitive means putting one or more words between *to* and the verb—e.g., to boldly go. In some cases, a strong argument can be made in favor of splitting the infinitive to promote readability (to *more than* double production). When splitting the infinitive helps readability, it is becoming increasingly acceptable to allow the split. Let functionality be your guide. If readability is not significantly improved by splitting the infinitive then don't.

> Split infinitive: The professor asked me *to* carefully *grade* the papers. (infinitive = to grade)
>
> Corrected: The professor asked me *to grade* the papers carefully.
>
> Split infinitive: The teacher asked him *to* independently *work* on the project. (infinitive = to work)
>
> Corrected: The teacher asked him *to work* independently on the project.
>
> Split infinitive: It was her first time on ice skates, and she wanted *to* slowly *go* around the rink. (infinitive = to go)

Corrected: It was her first time on ice skates, and she wanted *to go* around the rink slowly.

Parts of a Sentence

Clauses

Clauses are groups of words that work together in a sentence. Clauses may function as nouns, adjectives, or adverbs in a sentence. All clauses contain both a subject and a predicate. There are other groups of words that work together in sentences, but unless these word groups contain both a subject and a predicate, they are not considered clauses. Grammarians refer to "nonclauses" as phrases (see "Phrases," p. 107). Phrases may contain a subject or a verb but not both.

    Clause: as the store closed

    Phrase: at the store

    Clause: we went home

    Phrase: going home

Clauses are classified into two main categories depending on whether or not they make sense standing alone: (1) clauses that make sense standing alone are called independent, or main, clauses and (2) clauses that do not make sense standing alone are called dependent, or subordinate, clauses.

Independent Clause/Main Clause

3.41   The terms *independent clause* and *main clause* can be used interchangeably. Independent clauses make sense standing alone. An independent clause is a group of words that represent a complete thought and contain a subject and verb. Adding an initial capital and ending punctuation transforms an independent clause into a simple sentence. Many sentences consist of nothing but an independent clause; however, a sentence may also contain one or more dependent clauses and even additional independent clauses.

    Independent clause: it was a hot, humid day

    Independent clause: I needed a cool drink

    Two simple sentences: It was a hot, humid day. I needed a cool drink.

Note that by definition an independent clause is not a sentence. To be used as a sentence, an independent clause must begin with a capital letter and end with an appropriate punctuation mark.

Dependent Clause/Subordinate Clause

3.42   The terms *dependent clause* and *subordinate clause* can be used interchangeably. A subordinate clause does not represent a complete thought and cannot stand alone.

    Dependent clause: where my brother had gone

    Dependent clause: whom he was seeing

Dependent clauses must be combined with independent clauses in order to form sentences. In the sentences below, *we knew* and *we wondered* are independent clauses.

> Simple sentence: We knew *where my brother had gone.*
>
> Simple sentence: We wondered *whom he was seeing.*

For information on punctuating sentences containing independent and dependent clauses, see "Clauses and Punctuation," p. 127.

Distinguishing Between Dependent and Independent Clauses

3.43   Distinguishing between dependent and independent clauses is not as difficult as it may first appear.

> Independent clause: he had a cat
>
> Dependent clause: before he had a cat
>
> Independent clause: I ran the race
>
> Dependent clause: while I ran the race
>
> Independent clause: the car stalls
>
> Dependent clause: if the car stalls

The trick is to look at the first word in the clause. The clause is independent unless it begins with a subordinating conjunction or a relative pronoun.

subordinating conjunctions
after, although, as, as if, as much as, as though, because, before, even though, how, if, in order that, inasmuch as, provided, since, so that, than, that, though, unless, until, when, whenever, where, wherever, whether, which, while, who, whom, whose

relative pronouns
that, what, whatever, which, whichever, who, whoever, whom, whomever, whose, whosoever

To aid in spotting subordinating conjunctions, it is helpful to know that subordinating conjunctions are the only words in English that always begin clauses. In other words, subordinating conjunctions are always the first word in a clause (never the second word, third word, etc.). This tip is particularly helpful because there is another group of words that is sometimes confused with subordinating conjunctions: conjunctive adverbs.

conjunctive adverbs
accordingly, also, anyhow, anyway, as a result, besides, consequently, finally, first, for example, for instance, furthermore, hence, however, in addition, in conclusion, in fact, incidentally, indeed, instead, later, likewise, moreover, namely, nevertheless, on the contrary, otherwise, second, still, that is, therefore, to be sure, too

Like subordinating conjunctions, conjunctive adverbs act as transitional devices in sentences. Unlike subordinating conjunctions, however, conjunctive adverbs are the most movable of words in English. Also, conjunctive adverbs do not begin clauses. Consider the examples below.

> However, we know what to do.   We know, however, what to do.
>
> We know what to do, however.

In the first example above, it may appear that the conjunctive adverb *however* begins a subordinate clause, but notice in the second two examples that *however* is not actually part of the clause at all. *However* can function equally well at the beginning, middle, or end of a sentence. Use this test of movability to aid in distinguishing subordinating conjunctions from conjunctive adverbs.

(See "Subordinating Conjunctions," p. 90, "Relative Pronouns: Who and Whom," p. 96, and "Semicolon," p. 126 for more information.)

Phrases

In casual conversation, *phrase* refers to any group of words that function together. In the study of English, however, *phrase* has a more specific meaning, and we distinguish between phrases and clauses (see "Clauses," p. 105). All groups of words that function together are either clauses (which contain both a subject and a verb) or nonclauses (which do not contain both a subject and a verb); nonclauses are phrases. So a phrase is a group of words that act as a unit and contain either a subject or a verb but not both.

Phrases may function as nouns, verbs, or modifiers. Phrases may be located anywhere in a sentence, but when they begin a sentence, they are usually followed by a comma. Like dependent clauses, phrases cannot stand alone. If a phrase is not part of a complete sentence, it is a sentence fragment.

> *Walking to the park* was fun. (phrase functioning as a noun)
>
> The dog *was running* quickly. (phrase functioning as a verb)
>
> That is the prettiest flower *in the garden*. (phrase functioning as an adjective—modifies flower)
>
> We went *to the mall*. (phrase functioning as an adverb—modifies went)

Phrases tend to be confused with dependent clauses because neither of them forms a complete thought. Remember, a clause will have both a subject and a verb. A phrase will have one or the other but not both.

Absolute Phrase

3.44   The absolute phrase, or nominative absolute, is grammatically independent from the rest of the sentence. (In this case, "absolute" means independent or freewheeling.) The absolute phrase functions as a modifier without modifying any specific element in a sentence. The absolute phrase consists of a noun (or pronoun) followed by a participle. Absolute phrases may fall in any position in a sentence.

> *The plans having been made*, we went into the kitchen for coffee.
>
> The boy remembered her, *her hair blowing in the wind*.
>
> I followed the trail, *the dog leading the way*, until I came to the cabin.

USAGE   Agreement

Agreement: Noun with Plural Possessive Pronoun

4.1   The nouns that follow plural possessive pronouns may be singular or plural. Plural possessive pronouns used in a collective sense are followed by singular nouns; plural possessive pronouns used in a plural sense are followed by plural nouns.

Collective: My neighbors brought *their dog*. (more than one person, one dog)

Plural: The children brought *their dogs*. (more than one child, more than one dog)

Collective: We pushed *our car* to get it started. (more than one person, one car)

Plural: We moved *our chairs* closer to the fire. (more than one person, more than one chair)

When the noun following a plural possessive pronoun represents something abstract or figurative, the noun is frequently singular even when the pronoun is meant to have a plural sense.

Concrete noun: The council members took *their seats*.

Abstract noun: The council members maintained *their dignity* during the proceedings.

Concrete noun: The skaters laced *their skates*.

Figurative noun: The skaters waited for *their moment* on the ice.

See also Usage note under "Agreement: Pronoun with Antecedent," below.

Agreement: Pronoun with Antecedent

4.2   A pronoun must agree with its antecedent in number and gender. The antecedent is the noun or noun phrase to which the pronoun refers.

Sentence: *The kittens* chased the mouse. (replace *the kittens* with a pronoun)

Plural antecedent—plural pronoun: *They* chased the mouse.

Sentence: *The boy* flew a kite. (replace *the boy* with a pronoun)

Singular, masculine antecedent—singular, masculine pronoun: *He* flew a kite.

Be especially careful to make a possessive pronoun agree with its antecedent.

Correct: An artist is admired for her skill with a brush.

Incorrect: An artist is admired for their skill with a brush.

Usage note: The growing trend of using *their* to mean *his* or *her* has served to add confusion to the rules of agreement in number. When *their* is used incorrectly to mean *his* or *her,* it is frequently followed by a singular noun, as in the example below.

A teacher is responsible for *their classroom*.

We hear the construction above more frequently in conversation than the use of *their* as a plural possessive. This leads the ear to expect *their* to be followed by a singular noun.

Use *who* (or *that*) to refer to people and *which* (or *that*) to refer to objects. Either *who* or *which* can be used to refer to animals, depending on whether the animal is personified.

Incorrect: People which talk during movies annoy me.

Correct: People who talk during movies annoy me.

Correct: People that talk during movies annoy me.

Incorrect: The book who he is reading is a mystery novel.

Correct: The book that he is reading is a mystery novel.

Correct: The dog that runs through our yard is a nuisance.

Correct: Our dog, who never misses an opportunity to play, grabbed the towel I was using.

Correct: The cat which sat on the hearth looked quite content.

Agreement: Verb with Subject (Noun)

4.3   A subject and verb agree if they are both singular or both plural, that is, the subject and verb must agree in number.

Nouns are singular when they refer to one person, place, or thing and plural when they refer to more than one (cat—singular, cats—plural).

Most verbs ending in *s* are singular, while verbs not ending in *s* are plural. The exception to this general rule is verbs used with *I* and singular *you* (which takes the same verb form as plural *you*). Although *I* and *you* are singular, their verbs do not take an *s*: I go, you go, he goes, it goes, they go, we go.

The number of the subject is not affected by any phrases that fall between the subject and the verb. (See "Agreement: Verb with Indefinite Pronoun," p. 111, for the only exception.)

Sentence: The difficulties of going on a long trip were apparent.

Subject: the difficulties (plural)

Verb: were (plural)

The verb should agree with the subject, even when the subject and predicate are inverted.

Performing for the first time on this stage are the Lowell sisters. (subject = Lowell sisters, plural verb = are)

Performing for the first time on this stage is Winifred Lowell. (subject = Winifred Lowell, singular verb = is)

Agreement: Verb with Collective Subject

4.4   Collective nouns refer to groups: army, audience, band, chorus, class, clergy, club, committee, community, council, couple, crew, crowd, faculty, family, flock, fruit, gang, government, group, herd, jury, league, membership, mass, orchestra, pack, platoon, police, press, public, quartet, squad, staff, swarm, team, troop, varsity, etc.

A collective noun may take either a singular or plural verb depending on how the noun is used. If a collective noun is used to refer to a group as a whole, it will take a singular verb. If it refers to the members of a group, a plural verb is used.

Singular sense: The audience was restless.

Plural sense: The committee have been arguing among themselves.

Agreement: Pronoun with Collective Subject

4.5   A collective noun may take either a singular or a plural pronoun depending on how the noun is used.

Singular sense: The team announced its victory.

Plural sense: The class improved their scores.

Singular sense: Use all of your head.

Plural sense: Use all ten of your fingers.

Agreement: Verb with Compound Subject

4.6   Compound subjects are formed by joining words or groups of words with *and, or,* or *nor.*

Subjects joined with *and* take a plural verb. This rule is true whether the words making up the compound subject are singular or plural.

Single subject: Our cat spends a lot of time in the back yard.

Compound subject: Our cat and dog spend a lot of time in the back yard.

Compound subject: Our cats and dogs spend a lot of time in the back yard.

Compound subject: Our cat and dogs spend a lot of time in the back yard.

Compound subject: Our cats and dog spend a lot of time in the back yard.

Note that sometimes *and* is used as part of a phrase that functions as a unit to name a single item. In these cases, the subject is not a compound subject.

Example: Macaroni and cheese is my favorite dish.

Example: Stop and Go was the name of the market.

Singular subjects joined with *or* or *nor* take a singular verb.

Example: A chair or a stool fits under the counter.

Example: Either our cat or our dog sits on the couch.

Example: Neither Melissa nor Jody plays the clarinet.

When plural subjects are joined with *or* or *nor*, they take a plural verb.

Example: Jackets or sweaters are needed in the evenings.

Example: Either his parents or my parents take us to the pool.

Example: Neither our cats nor our dogs like to have baths.

When one or more plural subjects are joined to one or more singular subjects with *or* or *nor*, make the verb agree with the closer of the two subjects.

Example: A sports coat or evening clothes are required for the dinner party.

Example: Evening clothes or a sports coat is required for the dinner party.

Example: Either my parents or my aunt drives us to school.

Example: Either my aunt or my parents drive us to school.

Example: Neither the secretaries nor the supervisor was happy about the arrangement.

Example: Neither the supervisor nor the secretaries were happy about the arrangement.

Agreement: Personal Pronoun with Compound Subject

4.7   Compound subjects joined with *and* take plural pronouns.
Bryan and Ian took their dogs on a walk.

Compound subjects joined with *or* or *nor* take singular pronouns.
Neither Bryan nor Ian took his dog on a walk.

Difficulties can develop when the nouns in a compound subject joined with *or* or *nor* are of different genders.
Neither Bryan nor Lisa took his or her dog on a walk.

See "Agreement: Possessive Personal Pronoun with Indefinite Pronoun," below, for a discussion of gender issues with pronouns.

Agreement: Verb with Indefinite Pronoun

4.8   The verb must agree with the indefinite pronoun in number. Some of the indefinite pronouns take singular verbs, others take plural verbs, and others vary depending on context.

Singular: another, anybody, anyone, anything, each, each one, either, everybody, everyone, everything, much, neither, nobody, no one, one, other, somebody, someone, something
Everybody has a car.   Each of the parents has a car.

Plural: both, few, many, several
Both students have cars.   Several students have cars.

Vary (sometimes singular, sometimes plural): all, any, most, none, some
Most of the cars were dirty.   Most of the car was dirty.

Note that the indefinite pronouns that can be either singular or plural *(all, any, most, none, some)* constitute an exception to the standard rule of agreement that the number of the subject is not affected by any phrases that fall between the subject and the verb. When *all, any, most, none,* or *some* refer to a singular noun, they take a singular verb. When they refer to a plural noun, they take a plural verb.
Singular: *Some* of the paper *is* dry.
Plural: *Some* of the papers *are* on the desk.

Agreement: Possessive Personal Pronoun with Indefinite Pronoun

4.9   When indefinite pronouns serve as antecedents for pronouns, the personal pronoun must agree in number with the indefinite pronoun: singular indefinite pronouns take singular personal pronouns, plural indefinite pronouns take plural personal pronouns (see lists of singular and plural indefinite pronouns in "Agreement: Verb with Indefinite Pronoun," p. 111).

> Plural: *Some* have their own cars.
>
> Singular: *Each* has his or her own.

Agreement with indefinite pronouns does not sound difficult in theory, but agreement with the singular indefinite pronouns has become rather troublesome in practice because of the issue of gender. Indefinite pronouns do not reflect gender, but personal pronouns do. Consider the example that follows.

> Everybody in class brought his lunch on "bag day."

If everyone in class is not male, we may prefer the construction below.

> Everybody in class brought his or her lunch on "bag day."

Although accurate and grammatically correct, the construction above is awkward. Frequently, the resolution to this dilemma in spoken English is to use a plural personal pronoun as shown below.

> Everybody in class brought their lunch on "bag day."

There may come a time when using *their* to mean *his or her* is acceptable in standard English, but currently, such usage is still considered incorrect. The best solution in many cases may be to reword the sentence—use a noun rather than an indefinite pronoun.

> The students in class brought their lunches on "bag day."

Agreement: Adjective with Noun/Pronoun

4.10   An adjective and the noun or pronoun it modifies must agree in number.

> She has *two* brothers.
>
> Give me a piece. (articles *a* and *an* are adjectives)

When *this, that, these,* and *those* are used as adjectives, they must agree in number with the noun or pronoun that they are modifying.

> Singular: *this* bird, *that* alligator, *this* kind
>
> Plural: *these* sparrows, *those* crocodiles, *these* kinds

Clarity

4.11   Grammatical structure and punctuation can enhance communication or, if used improperly, obscure meaning. See "Pronouns—Clear Reference," p. 92, and "Comma—To avoid ambiguity," p. 121.

Parallel Structure

A sentence is parallel when equal or closely related ideas are expressed by grammatical elements of equal rank (nouns paired with nouns, phrases paired with phrases, clauses paired with clauses, etc.). Parallel structure adds clarity, smoothness, and polish to writing. There are three situations in which parallel construction should always be used: (1) constructions using coordinating conjunctions, (2) constructions using correlative conjunctions, and (3) constructions comparing or contrasting elements.

Coordinating Constructions

4.12   When two or more ideas are joined by a coordinating conjunction (for, and, nor, but, or, yet, so), each of the ideas should be in the same grammatical form (part of speech).

> Not parallel: The dog was *short, fat,* and *had a lot of hair.* (two adjectives and a verb phrase)
>
> Parallel: The dog was *short, fat,* and *hairy.* (all adjectives)
>
> Not parallel: We went *sailing* and *on a picnic.* (gerund and prepositional phrase)
>
> Parallel: We went *sailing* and *picnicking.* (two gerunds)
>
> Not Parallel: Cost is how much is paid, and payback is how much people are getting.
>
> Parallel: Cost is how much is paid, and payback is how much is received.

See "Coordinating Conjunctions," p. 88, for more information.

Correlative Constructions

4.13   The correlative conjunctions (both…and, either…or, not only…but also, etc.) should join grammatical elements of equal weight.

> Not parallel: The cat was both *finicky* and *did not obey well.* (adjective and verb phrase)
>
> Parallel: The cat was both *finicky* and *disobedient.* (two adjectives)

See "Correlative Conjunctions," p. 89, for more information.

Comparing and Contrasting Constructions

4.14   When two or more ideas are compared or contrasted, each idea should be the same part of speech.

> Not parallel: *Basketball* no longer interests me as much as *to watch soccer.* (noun and infinitive)
>
> Parallel: *Basketball* no longer interests me as much as *soccer.* (two nouns)
>
> Parallel: *To watch basketball* no longer interests me as much as *to watch soccer.* (two infinitives)
>
> Not parallel: He is known more for his *showmanship* than for *what he has done in athletics.* (noun and clause)
>
> Parallel: He is known more for his *showmanship* than for his *athleticism.* (two nouns)
>
> Not parallel: *Playing* ball is more fun than *to do* homework. (gerund and infinitive)
>
> Parallel: *Playing* ball is more fun than *doing* homework. (two gerunds)

Problems with Modifiers

Improper use or placement of modifiers can cause confusion for readers. This confusion can range from momentary uncertainty about the writer's meaning to inability to discern the writer's meaning at all. However, modifiers gone astray can also add humor to the serious business of English grammar, as in the examples below.

> Riding my new mountain bike, the neighbor's dog chased me down the street.
>
> The man basted the chicken wearing an apron.

Misplaced Modifiers

4.15   Modifiers describe, define, clarify, or provide more explicit information about the words they modify. There is nothing intrinsic to the modifiers themselves that shows which word they modify; therefore, modifiers must be carefully placed in sentences so that it is clear which words they modify. Modifiers are said to be misplaced when it is unclear which word they modify or when they modify the wrong word. In general, modifiers should be placed as close as possible to the words they modify. Frequently, misplaced modifiers can be corrected simply by moving the ambiguous phrase closer to the word it modifies.

> Misplaced: I spoke with the woman who is standing by the potted palm in the yellow dress.

In the example above, the reader may think that the palm is draped in a yellow dress. Correct this confusion by relocating the modifier.

> Corrected: I spoke with the woman in the yellow dress who is standing by the potted palm.

Now there is no confusion over who is wearing the yellow dress. In the example below, there is some confusion over who is in the back of the truck.

> Misplaced: He took the dog when he left this morning in the back of the truck.
>
> Corrected: When he left this morning, he took the dog in the back of the truck.

Now it is clear who is riding in the back of the truck.

Dangling Modifiers

4.16   Dangling modifiers occur when a modifying phrase or clause does not clearly modify a word in the sentence or seems to clearly modify a word other than the one the writer intended. A dangling modifier usually appears at the beginning of a sentence, and the word that it should be modifying either is not in the sentence or is not the grammatical subject (as opposed to the implied subject) of the sentence. When a modifier dangles, the actual, literal meaning of the sentence is far different from the meaning the writer intended.

Introductory participial phrases are common culprits for dangling and are referred to as dangling participles.

> Dangling: Walking across the parking lot, her purse strap broke.
>
> Corrected: Walking across the parking lot, she felt her purse strap break.
>
> Corrected: While she was walking across the parking lot, her purse strap broke.

In the first example shown, the introductory participial phrase modifies "her purse strap." Since her purse strap could not possibly have been walking across the parking lot, the sentence must be rephrased so that either the noun that the participial phrase is modifying follows it directly or the participial phrase is changed to an adverb clause. Below is another example of a dangling participle.

Dangling: Newly renovated, we enjoyed traveling the road. (phrase modifies the subject *we*)

Corrected: We enjoyed traveling the newly renovated road.

It is not just participial phrases, however, that can dangle. Other introductory phrases can also be left dangling when the grammatical subject of the sentence is not the word that the phrase is intended to modify.

Dangling: By leaving early for the concert, good seats were assured. (phrase modifies the subject *seats*)

Corrected: By leaving early for the concert, we assured ourselves of good seats.

Dangling: Alone in the building, the wind rattling the windows terrified her. (phrase modifies the subject *wind*)

Corrected: Alone in the building, she was terrified by the wind rattling the windows.

Dangling: After jogging a mile, a drink of water was all I wanted. (phrase modifies the subject *drink*)

Corrected: After jogging a mile, all I wanted was a drink of water.

Dangling: While swimming in the pool, my neighbor was seen pruning her roses. (phrase modifies the subject *neighbor*)

Corrected: While swimming in the pool, I saw my neighbor pruning her roses.

Dangling: To explore the Grand Canyon, a hike to the bottom is recommended. (phrase modifies the subject *hike*)

Corrected: To explore the Grand Canyon, you should hike to the bottom.

The easiest way to deal with dangling modifiers is to figure out what word the phrase should be modifying and then make sure that word is the grammatical subject of the sentence.

Terminal Participles

4.17   Participial phrases are such useful modifiers that there is a tendency to use them where they don't belong. Participial phrases are always adjectives and like all adjectives they must modify a noun or pronoun. Adjectives cannot modify phrases or clauses. When a participial phrase is used at the end of a sentence (terminal participle), the phrase must modify either the noun just preceding it or the subject of the sentence. In the examples below, note the use of the comma to show whether the participial phrase is with the word it modifies (no comma) or is removed from that word (comma).

He ran the course *zigzagging up the hill*. (modifies *course*)

He ran the course, *singing as he went*. (modifies *he*)

Participial phrases cannot be used to modify concepts. In the first two sentences below, the terminal participle was intended to modify the concept of running rivers. In actuality, however, the participial phrase modifies either the noun directly preceding it (as in the first example below) or the subject (as in the second example). The corrected example states the intended meaning.

> Incorrect: He was running rivers in a kayak *adding adventure to his life.* (modifies *kayak*)

> Incorrect: He was running rivers in a kayak, *adding adventure to his life.* (modifies *he*)

> Correct: Running rivers in a kayak added adventure to his life.

Special (Confused) Word Pairs/Incorrect Word for Context

4.18   In this level of *Editor in Chief®*, we focus on the following confused pairs of words:

affect (most commonly used as a verb meaning "to influence"; in psychology may also be used as a noun meaning "emotion") / effect (most commonly used as a noun meaning "the result"; may also be used as a verb meaning "to cause")

accept (receive) / except (excluding)

affective (emotional) / effective (having an intended result)

among (used with collective quantities: argument between members) / between (used with distinct quantities: argument between Bob, Joan, and Ned)

anxious (uneasy, apprehensive) / eager (earnestly desiring something)

are (form of verb to be) / our (possessive of first person plural)

as (used when followed by a verb: "We left at 1:00 as planned.") / like (used when followed by a noun: "The boy ran like the wind.")

can (to be able to) / may (to be permitted to)

conscious (aware) / conscience (a sense of right and wrong)

could have / could of: *of* should not be used for *have*

disinterested (impartial) / uninterested (indifferent)

eminent (standing out) / imminent (about to happen)

farther (used to refer to physical distance: "5 miles farther") / further (used to refer to abstract distance: "to gain further understanding")

fewer or few (used with countable plural nouns: "9 items or fewer") / less or little (used with singular nouns not easily counted: "less rain than expected")

impeccable (flawless) / implacable (impossible to please)

imply (to suggest without stating directly) / infer (derive a conclusion)

inhabited (lived in) / inhibited (suppressed or held back)

lay (transitive verb meaning to put or place) / lie (intransitive verb meaning to rest or recline)

raise (to move to a higher position, to elevate—transitive verb—you raise objects) / rise (to move from lower to higher—intransitive verb—people/objects rise on their own)

selective (discriminating) / selected (chosen)

Note: for information on "could care less," see CONTENT, p. 83.

Unnecessary Words

4.19   Unnecessary words should be deleted.

Negatives: Use only one negative word to state a negative idea.

    Incorrect: We don't have no bananas.

    Correct: We don't have any bananas.

    Correct: We have no bananas.

The words *hardly* and *scarcely* are also considered negative words and should not be used with other negatives.

    Incorrect: We have hardly no bananas.

    Correct: We have hardly any bananas.

    Correct: We have no bananas.

Some words are excessive or repetitive and should be deleted.

    Incorrect: The thing is is the people are hungry.

    Correct: The people are hungry. (or The thing is, the people are hungry.)

    Incorrect: Rover he ran away.

    Correct: Rover ran away. (or He ran away.)

    Incorrect: We are, like, hungry!

    Correct: We are hungry!

Subject: Use a noun or pronoun (not both) as subject.

    Incorrect: Marnie she had a lovely coat.

    Correct: Marnie had a lovely coat.

    Correct: She had a lovely coat.

PUNCTUATION

Apostrophe

5.1   Use an apostrophe in contractions to show where letters or numbers have been left out.

    could not = couldn't   let us = let's   it is = it's

    the 1990s = the '90s

Note that *its* (without apostrophe) is the possessive form of *it*. (See "Homonyms," p. 129.)

5.2   Use an apostrophe to form the plural of letters, but do not use an apostrophe to form the plural of numbers.

    Mind your p's and q's.

    Shakespeare lived in the late 1500s and early 1600s.

Usage note: At one time, forming the plural of numbers by adding apostrophe *s* was common; however, in current style manuals, the preference is to drop the apostrophe. If you wish to use an apostrophe when forming plural numbers, note that under no circumstances is the construction '90's considered correct.

5.3 Use an apostrophe to form the possessive, not the plural, of a word.

5.4 Add *'s* to form the singular possessive. (An exception is the possessive form of *it*—see "Apostrophe" [5.1], p. 117.)

dog's bone   Maria's ball   car's color

one year's time   brother-in-law's family the water's edge

5.5 Add an apostrophe to form the possessive of a plural ending in *-s*, *-es*, or *-ies*.

cats' toys   foxes' holes   butterflies' flowers

board of directors' meeting   five cents' worth   two weeks' vacation

parentheses' location   analyses' results

5.6 Add *'s* to form the possessive of plural nouns that do not end in *s*.

women's hats   sheep's wool   children's toys   tomorrow's news

bacteria's virulence feet's position phenomena's occurrence

5.7 Add *'s* to form the possessive of indefinite pronouns.

anyone's idea   everybody's school   someone's gloves   someone else's love

Usage note: Possessive pronouns do not use an apostrophe to form the possessive. See "Pronouns," p. 92.

Apostrophes are unnecessary with the regular plurals of words (*the parents of the boys*).

Colon

5.8 Use a colon between numbers indicating hours and minutes.

We will arrive at 9:15.

5.9 A colon follows the greeting in a business letter.

Dear Sir: Dear Dr. Martinez:

5.10 Use a colon to introduce a list of items.

We needed three things at the market: milk, flour, and eggs.

5.11 Use a colon with *as follows* and *the following* when the example immediately follows.

He gave us the following example of a typical fall Saturday in the yard: rake the leaves, mow the lawn, and enjoy a cold drink in the lounge chair.

5.12 Use a colon to introduce a clause or phrase that explains, restates, illustrates, or provides more information about the preceding clause.

He was always unique: the only time he wore matching socks was on "clash day."

The last hope of many endangered species may be zoo breeding programs: captive breeding of endangered animals that are then released into the wild.

5.13 Usage note: Style manuals recommend that an independent clause precede a colon and that a colon not fall between a verb and its objects.

Incorrect: His backpack contained: books, binders, and his lunch.

Correct: His backpack contained books, binders, and his lunch.

Correct: His backpack contained the following: books, binders, and his lunch.

Correct: His backpack contained three types of items: books, binders, and his lunch.

5.14   The colon always falls outside quotation marks or parentheses.

We went to see "Taming of the Shrew": it is my favorite play.

While preparing for the expedition, they told us to beware of the following (if we still wanted to go after reading the list): poisonous snakes, malarial mosquitoes, parasitic worms, dysentery amoeba.

Comma

Conventional Uses

5.15   Use a comma to separate the elements of an address (street and city, city and state), but do not use a comma to separate the ZIP code.

5 Elm Street, Sample Town, New York   Monterey, CA 93940

5.16   Use a comma after the state in a sentence when using the format city, state.

We are going to Sample Town, New York, to visit our grandmother.

5.17   Use a comma in dates between day and year in the format month, day, year.

January 10, 1996   April 5, 2001

Usage note: If you follow the European model, write 9 May 1999—
                    no commas.

5.18   Use a comma after the year in a sentence when using the format month, day, year.

We have to be in Nevada on January 10, 1996, in order to visit our friends.

5.19   Use a comma after the greeting of a friendly letter.

Dear Emilio,

Usage note: Business letters use a colon after the salutation.

5.20   Use a comma to separate a name and title when the title immediately follows the name.

Randall Brown, Principal   Lois Gonzalez, Manager

5.21   Use a comma after the closing of a letter.

Sincerely,   With best wishes,   Love,

Items in a Series

5.22   Use a comma between words or phrases in a series.

blue, red, and green   up the hill, over the log, and down the hole

Usage note: Some sources may consider the comma before *and*
                    optional. For the purpose of consistency in this series,
                    include the comma before *and*.

5.23   Commas are sometimes used between short, parallel independent clauses.

We came, we saw, we ate.

Mom went to dinner, Dad played golf, and I stayed home.

Usage note: Commas are not used between independent clauses
                    that are neither short nor parallel when the clauses are

not separated by coordinating conjunctions. This error is known as comma splice or comma fault. See "Semicolon," p. 126, for more information.

5.24 Use a comma to separate coordinate adjectives (adjectives that equally modify a noun).

> She had a warm, friendly smile.

Usage note: See "Coordinate and Noncoordinate Modifiers," p. 85, for more information.

Introductory Elements

5.25 Use a comma to separate an introductory word or interjection from the rest of the sentence.

> Yes, I have heard of that TV show.   Hey, did you see that comet?
>
> Well, I guess that's true.

5.26 Use commas to set off an introductory phrase or dependent clause that precedes a main clause unless the introductory phrase or clause immediately precedes the main verb.

> After we left, she phoned the office.
>
> From the couch, the cat jumped onto the bookcase.
>
> On the water lay a fifty-foot schooner.

Usage note: Dependent clauses are also referred to as subordinate clauses. See "Subordinating Conjunctions," p. 90, for more information.

Interrupters/Nonessential Elements

5.27 Use commas to separate nouns of address from the rest of the sentence.

> Kim, I asked you to step over here.
>
> You know, Rebecca, we could go to the store tomorrow.

5.28 Use commas to set off sentence interrupters.

> The recent game, on the other hand, showed the wisdom of working on plays.
>
> He had told us, however, that he would study more.

5.29 Set off nonessential appositives (a noun or noun/pronoun phrase next to a noun, which identifies, defines, or explains the noun) with commas.

> The tomato, or "love apple," was first cultivated in Central America.
>
> The Marsdens, our nearest neighbors, left on vacation today.
>
> My brother's dog, the big white one, is rolling in the leaves.
>
> Her oldest brother, Jim, is leaving for college tomorrow.

5.30 Usage note: There is often confusion about when to set off people's names or the titles of books, movies, etc. with commas. If the name or title specifies which person, book, etc. is being referred to, then it is essential to the meaning of the sentence and should not be set off with commas. In the last example above, we have already specified that her "oldest brother" is leaving for college. His name is not essential to the meaning of the sentence (since she can only have one oldest brother) and so we set off his name with commas. Consider these examples.

> Her brother, Jim, is leaving for college tomorrow. (She only has one brother, so the name is not essential to the meaning of the sentence.)

> Her brother Jim is leaving for college tomorrow. (She has more than one brother, and it is Jim who is leaving tomorrow. Jim's name specifies which brother is leaving and is, therefore, essential to the meaning of the sentence.)

5.31 Set off nonessential (nonrestrictive) phrases or clauses with commas.

> The dog, who always had a mind of his own, started shedding in January.

Usage note: See "Clauses and Punctuation," p. 127, for more information.

5.32 Use commas to set off absolute phrases.

> She stared at the gray water, her face set in harsh lines.

> The day fading into dusk, he took his leave.

Usage note: See "Absolute Phrase," p. 107, for more information on absolute phrases.

5.33 Use commas to set off modifying phrases that do not immediately precede the word or phrase they modify; for example, in the first sentence below, *the* falls between the modifiers and the noun they modify.

> Old and venerable, the oak had stood for 75 years.

> I stuffed the family cats, both highly vocal about their predicament, into the cat carrier.

5.34 Use commas to set off contrasting expressions within a sentence.

> She turned 27, not 25, on her last birthday.

> He likes jazz, not rock and roll.

5.35 Use a comma to introduce a direct question.

> He wanted to ask, Where are you from?

> The question is, Does he really want the job?

To avoid ambiguity or misreading

5.36
> I stayed with my brother, and my sister and my aunt went skiing.

> Sally spoke to Ruth, and Tom spoke to George.

> I told Mary, Jane was missing.

> What I say I will do, I do.

> He stood against the wall, towering over his friends.

See also "Terminal Participles," p. 115.

With Conjunctions

5.37 Use commas before coordinating conjunctions joining two independent clauses.

We took the bus, but she will take the train.
My sister mowed the lawn, and I raked the leaves.

Usage note: See "Conjunctions," p. 88, for more information.

5.38 Use a comma after a conjunctive adverb.

I don't like what you say; however, I support your right to say it.

(See also "Distinguishing Between Dependent and Independent Clauses," p. 106.)

With Quotation Marks

5.39 Use a comma to separate a direct quote from a phrase identifying the speaker.

Tomas said, "We had fun doing English today."

"We had fun doing English today," Tomas said.

"Go to the third rock," the game manual read. (virtual "speaker" in this case)

5.40 Place commas inside ending quotation marks.

The package was marked "fragile," but the contents were quite sturdy.

"We had fun," he said.

Usage note: We have noted some confusion over this particular rule, possibly because British usage differs from American usage. American style manuals, however, are all in agreement: commas and periods always go inside closing quotation marks. There is an interesting story about this punctuation style. It is said that when typesetting began in America, the lead used to make the type was not as refined as that used in England, and the printers had problems with the small commas and periods outside the quotation marks breaking off. To solve this problem, they moved the commas and periods inside the quotation marks! In American punctuation, the periods and commas go inside the quotation marks while the larger colons and semicolons go outside the quotation marks.

When *Not* to Use Commas

5.41 Commas are sometimes used inappropriately. Below are some of the more common errors in comma usage. No comma should be used

a between the month and year in a sentence

Incorrect: We will visit Georgia in July, 1996.

b when all items in a series are joined by *or* or *and*

Incorrect (delete both commas): We went sledding, and skating, and skiing.

Incorrect (delete both commas): I don't know Gerard, or Manuel, or Alan.

c with noncoordinate adjectives

Incorrect: I saw a big, orange cat under the porch.

d after a dependent phrase or clause just before the main verb

Incorrect: On the floor, lay a bat.

e   between a subject and its verb
Incorrect: The chairman of the arts, told the committee to vote.

f   before a subordinating conjunction (dependent clause/main clause)
Incorrect: He ran into the house, because it started raining.

g   to separate adjectives and adverbs joined by *but*
Incorrect: a car with plush, but costly upholstery
Incorrect (delete 2nd comma): he fell, reaching for a branch, but missing

h   with a compound predicate
Incorrect: The barking dog chased the mailman, and bit him.

i   with an essential clause, phrase, or appositive
Incorrect: The manager quit, because she was planning to move.
Incorrect: He mowed the yard, in exchange for a meal.
Incorrect: The American, Rita, is coming. (unless there is only one American)

j   to separate adverbs or an adverb phrase
Incorrect: He turned the knob left, and right.
Incorrect (delete 2nd comma): None of them won, although, they were all good.

k   to separate a dependent clause
Incorrect: The room was filled with chairs used so often, that they were rickety.

l   when dependent clause follows main clause
Incorrect: He will see us, if he comes.

m   to separate compound objects
Incorrect: Lift your arms, and legs.

n   between two independent clauses not separated by a coordinating conjunction (see "Run-on Sentences and Comma Splices," p. 129).

o   between dependent clauses
Incorrect: She thinks that she is ugly, and that they dislike her.

(See also "Clauses and Punctuation," p. 127.)

Exclamation Point

5.42   Use an exclamation point after an exclamatory sentence.
Stop that dog!   We know what to do!   I love chocolate!

5.43   Use an exclamation point after an interjection that stands alone.
Stop! Don't you know to look both ways before crossing a street?

Usage note: An interjection that begins a sentence may function as an introductory word and may be set off from the sentence with a comma instead of an exclamation point; for example, Hey, wait for me!

5.44   Place the exclamation point inside quotation marks at the end of a quoted exclamation.
Incorrect: "Get that snake off the counter"! screamed Jamie.
Correct: "Get that snake off the counter!" screamed Jamie.

5.45 Usage note: In contrast to commas and periods (which always fall inside closing quotation marks), an exclamation point falls inside closing quotation marks only when it applies to what is inside the quotation marks. If it is not part of the quoted material, it goes outside the quotation marks; for example, That box is marked "fragile"!

5.46 Place the exclamation point within closing parentheses when the exclamation point applies to the word, phrase, or clause within the parentheses. When the exclamation point applies to the sentence rather than the parenthetical material, it falls outside the closing parenthesis.

In our house, Thanksgiving lasts two weeks. (Great, Mom, turkey goulash, how original!)

It took us three days to requisition the materials (one day for shipping and two days to fill out forms!).

Ronald gave a flawless performance (if you ignored the minor slip-ups)!

Usage note: Unlike periods and question marks, which have standard usage, use of exclamation points is at the discretion of the writer. In the examples above, the positions of the exclamation points show what the writer wished to emphasize.

Hyphen

5.47 Use a hyphen with compound numbers.

twenty-five   ninety-four   forty-three

5.48 Use a hyphen to create temporary compound adjectives (unit modifiers). See "Compound Adjectives," p. 86.

half-baked plan   six-year-old boy   much-loved doll

Parentheses

5.49 Use parentheses (in pairs) to enclose "parenthetic information" (phrases and clauses that add information or explanations).

My favorite exhibit at the aquarium was the sea otters (*Enhydra lutris*).

5.50 If an entire sentence is enclosed within parentheses, then the period should also fall within the parentheses. However, if the parentheses enclose an independent clause that is part of a longer sentence, the independent clause should not end in a period.

My neighbor got a new cat. (She already has three others.)

My neighbor's new cat (she already has three others) is orange.

5.51 A question mark or exclamation point may be used with a parenthetic element that is part of a longer sentence.

My aunt (poor woman!) is now supporting her son and his three children.

After waiting in line for two hours to get advance tickets, we found (who could have known?) that there was no line at all at the gate and plenty of tickets remaining.

Period

5.52 Use a period to end a declarative sentence. See also "Run-on Sentences," p. 129.

> A sentence begins with a capital letter and ends with a punctuation mark.

5.53 Use a period after abbreviations and initials.

> Washington, D.C.   Dr. Nolan   Mr. J. Pedrewski

Usage Note: It is becoming more acceptable to use some common abbreviations without periods, e.g., mph, km, etc. However, for the purposes of consistency in this series, use the periods with abbreviations.

5.54 Always place periods inside closing quotation marks.

> We delivered a package marked "fragile."

See usage note under "Comma—With Quotation Marks," p. 122.

5.55 A period falls within closing parentheses only if the entire sentence is within the parentheses. If the parentheses enclose material that is part of a longer sentence, the period (or other punctuation ending the sentence) falls outside the parentheses.

> He said that the dog ate the liver off his plate (he didn't say how the dog got the liver in the first place).

> The physics professor used humor to enliven his lectures. (In fact, we suspected that he really wanted to be a comedian.)

Question Mark

5.56 Use a question mark after a direct question (interrogative sentence).

> Are we there yet?   What time is it?

5.57 Do not use a question mark with a statement or indirect question.

> I wondered if I could do that.   We asked him how he liked the play.

5.58 Place a question mark inside the quotation marks after a quoted question.

> "What day is soccer practice?" asked Lucia.

5.59 Usage note: Again in contrast to commas and periods (which always fall inside closing quotation marks), a question mark falls inside closing quotation marks only when it applies to what is inside the quotation marks. In the following example, the question mark applies to the entire sentence, not to the word inside the quotation marks: Is that box marked "fragile"?

Quotation Marks, Double

5.60 Use quotation marks to enclose direct quotes (include both parts of a divided quotation).

> "I need help on this English paper," said Grover.

> "This beautiful day," said Mark, "is too good to waste indoors."

5.61 Do not use quotation marks with indirect quotes.

He said that it was a beautiful day.

5.62 When a direct quote is longer than one paragraph, place quotation marks only at the beginning of each paragraph and at the end of the last paragraph. (The following example is quoted from *The Story of English* by McCrum, Cran, and MacNeil.)

"Shakespeare is universal in his appeal and sympathy not least because he wrote in a language that has become global....

"He was a country boy, born in Stratford, in the heart of Warwickshire, then a town of some 1500 inhabitants."

5.63 Use quotation marks on the titles of songs, stories, poems, articles, book chapters, or television shows.

We have to memorize "Jabberwocky" by Thursday.

5.64 Use quotation marks to set off unusual words/phrases or words/ phrases used in unusual ways.

She had a "punny" sense of humor.

He was a "dinner at eight" kind of guy.

Quotation Marks, Single

5.65 Single quotation marks are used to enclose a quotation within a quotation.

"I always thought his 'poor me' attitude was an act," Eugenie said.

5.66 When single and double quotation marks appear together, punctuation that normally would fall within the double quotation marks should fall within both the single and double quotation marks.

Heather said, "Before the game, our coach told us 'United we stand; divided we fall.'"

5.67 Usage note: The rules for usage of other punctuation (e.g., period, comma) with quotation marks apply to single quotation marks as well as to double quotation marks.

Semicolon

5.68 A semicolon is used between closely related independent clauses that are not joined by a coordinating conjunction.

The dog dreamed on the porch; the neighbor's cat slipped quietly along the porch rail.

5.69 Use a semicolon between independent clauses joined by conjunctive adverbs. Adverbs that serve as conjunctions include accordingly, also, anyhow, anyway, besides, consequently, finally, first, furthermore, hence, however, incidentally, indeed, instead, later, likewise, moreover, namely, nevertheless, otherwise, second, still, that is, therefore, and too. Some prepositional phrases and infinitives also function as conjunctive adverbs: as a result, for example, for instance, in addition, in conclusion, in fact, on the contrary, to be sure.

She always had a strong sense of style; in fact, she became a highly regarded decorator.

5.70 Use semicolons to separate items in a series when the items themselves use commas.

> The team consisted of both national and international players: Peter Schmeichel, goal keeper, Denmark; Ryan Giggs, left wing, Wales; Steve Bruce, center back and captain, England.

5.71 Semicolons fall outside parentheses.

> We wanted to go on an exotic vacation (at least I did); however, the only vacation spot we could afford was Disney World.

5.72 Semicolons fall outside quotation marks.

> She had said the place was really "original"; I wasn't expecting black lights and purple walls.

See also "Run-On Sentences," p. 129.

Multiple Punctuation

5.73 In general, two marks of punctuation should not be used together except in the cases of brackets, parentheses, quotation marks, ellipses, and dashes.

> Incorrect: What was her expression when you said, "I know you did it."?
> Correct: What was her expression when you said, "I know you did it"?

Clauses and Punctuation

Recognizing dependent and independent clauses is useful when one is punctuating sentences. In some instances, commas are required between dependent and independent clauses, and in other cases, they are not. Following are a few simple rules of thumb for when to use commas in sentences containing clauses:

5.74 independent clause + independent clause =

> comma after the first clause when the clauses are joined by a coordinating conjunction
>
> Example: The sun was shining brightly, and the weather was warm.

5.75 independent clause + independent clause =

> semicolon after the first clause when the clauses are not joined by a coordinating conjunction
>
> Example: The sun was shining brightly; the weather was warm.

5.76 dependent clause + independent clause =

> comma after the dependent clause
>
> Example: After we left for the country, the package we were waiting for arrived.

5.77 independent clause + dependent clause =

> usually no comma, however, this varies depending on whether the dependent clause is restrictive (essential) or nonrestrictive (nonessential)

5.78 independent clause + dependent clause (when dependent clause immediately precedes main verb) =

> no comma
>
> Example: Only after we had studied did we take the test.

5.79   (independent clause +) dependent clause + dependent clause =
no comma

Example: He knows that he is smart and that he is handsome.

For more on the difference between restrictive (essential) and nonrestrictive (nonessential) see "Essential vs. Nonessential," below.

To aid in remembering some general rules for punctuating clauses, think of them as follows:

I + I = comma or semicolon

I + D = no comma

D + I = comma

Note that the rules above apply to clauses, not phrases. For more on the difference between clauses and phrases, see pages 105–107.

See "Comma," p. 119, and "Semicolon," p. 126, for more information on punctuating clauses.

Essential vs. Nonessential

5.80   Restrictive (essential) clauses or phrases are essential to the meaning of the sentence. Removing them would change the meaning of the sentence. Nonrestrictive (nonessential) clauses or phrases can be removed without altering the meaning of the sentence; they give additional or incidental information which is not essential to the basic idea that the sentence is conveying.

Nonrestrictive (nonessential): Our neighbor, who is sitting in that chair by the wall, is well-liked in our community.

Restrictive (essential): The man who is sitting in that chair by the wall is our neighbor.

Consider the difference in meaning of the two examples below.

Nonrestrictive (nonessential): The girl, who is wearing a very odd hat, stood indecisively before the classroom door.

Restrictive (essential): The girl who is wearing a very odd hat stood indecisively before the classroom door.

In the first example above, the girl who is the subject of the sentence is the only girl standing in front of the door, and we are given incidental information about her. In the second example, there are other girls standing in front of the door, and we are given information to help us identify to which girl the sentence refers.

To test a phrase or clause to see whether it is essential or nonessential, imagine that the commas are handles that you can use to lift the phrase or clause out of the sentence. If the basic meaning of the sentence does not change, then the phrase or clause is nonessential and should be set off with commas. If the basic meaning of the sentence changes, then the phrase or clause is essential and should not be set off with commas.

The general punctuation trend is toward using fewer commas, and this trend is noticeable with nonessential clauses. In cases where nonessential clauses do not seem obviously parenthetical, the clauses are increasingly not set off with commas. For example, nonessential clauses beginning with *while* or *whereas* frequently do not take commas unless the clauses are long. In the examples below, both punctuation patterns shown for the nonessential clause will be commonly seen.

> Essential: She finally ate her dinner while the baby was sleeping.
> Nonessential: She likes coffee while her friend prefers tea.
> Nonessential: She likes coffee, while her friend prefers tea.

As a rule of thumb, commas are usually used with nonessential clauses beginning with *who*, *which*, *where*, or *when*.

Run-on Sentences and Comma Splices

5.81   Run-on sentences and comma splices may be corrected by using a semicolon, conjunction (coordinating or subordinating), or colon or by creating two sentences. In this level of *Editor in Chief*®, the answer key shows the best answers based on the context; however, there may be acceptable answers that are not shown.

> Incorrect (run on): Bob played his harp he was rehearsing for tonight's performance.
> Incorrect (comma splice): Bob played his harp, he was rehearsing for tonight's performance.
> Correct: Bob played his harp. He was rehearsing for tonight's performance.
> Correct: Bob played his harp; he was rehearsing for tonight's performance.
> Correct: Bob played his harp: he was rehearsing for tonight's performance.
> Correct: Bob played his harp because he was rehearsing for tonight's performance.

Sentence Fragments

5.82   In this level of *Editor in Chief*®, the answer key corrects sentence fragments by joining the sentence fragment to a complete sentence.

> Incorrect: The bird was sitting on the roof. Sunning himself.
> Correct: The bird was sitting on the roof, sunning himself.

Note that a sentence fragment may also be corrected by rewriting the sentence in other ways, as shown below.

> Possible: Sunning himself, the bird sat on the roof.

SPELLING

Homonyms

6.1   In this level of *Editor in Chief*®, we focus on the following homonyms:

in to/into	stationary/stationery
its/it's	their/they're/there
hear/here	to/too/two
metal/mettle	we/wee

principal/principle   whose/who's
sole/soul   your/you're

Note: some words that sound similar are listed under "Special (Confused) Word Pairs/Incorrect Word for Context," p. 116.

Plurals

6.2   Some words have the same form for the singular and plural.

sheep   deer

6.3   The plurals of words that end in the sound of *f* are usually formed by changing the *f* to *v* and adding *-es*. There are, however, exceptions.

leaf/leaves   knife/knives   roof/roofs

6.4   The plurals of words that end in *y* are usually formed by changing the *y* to *i* and adding *-es*.

berry/berries   carry/carries

6.5   Some nouns have unusual plural spellings (e.g., *es* replaces *is*, *a* replaces *on*)

analysis/analyses   criterion/criteria   phenomenon/phenomena

Possessives

See "Apostrophe," p. 117.

Closed and Open Spellings

6.6   In general, verb phrases consisting of a verb + preposition are open (two words, no hyphen). The same two words are combined when functioning as a noun.

clean up: verb phrase / cleanup: noun

pick up: verb phrase / pickup: noun

Other open/closed spellings follow:

care less: verb phrase / careless: adjective

a lot: a lot is always two words (never alot)

all right: unlike already (all ready), all right is always two words (never alright)

Miscellaneous Spellings

6.7   The following miscellaneous spelling words appear in errored form in this edition of *Editor in Chief*®:

endurance   receive

intrigued   rigorous

nucleus   through

played